Almost Fat Free Down-Home Cooking

Heavenly Tasting Food with

Just a Touch of Devil in It

Doris Cross

PRIMA PUBLISHING

Nutritional Analyses

A per serving nutritional breakdown is provided for each recipe. If a range is given for an ingredient amount, the breakdown is based on the smaller number. If a range is given for servings, the breakdown is based on the larger number. If a choice of ingredients is given in an ingredient listing, the breakdown is calculated using the first choice. Nutritional content may vary depending on the specific brands or types of ingredients used. "Optional" ingredients or those for which no specific amount is stated are not included in the breakdown.

Previously published under the title *Fat Free 2* by Prima Publishing, 1995.

PRIMA PUBLISHING and colophon are registered trademarks of Prima Communications, Inc.

Library of Congress Cataloging-in-Publication Data

Cross, Doris
    Almost fat free down-home cooking : heavenly tasting food with
      just a touch of devil in it / Doris Cross.
      p.   cm.
    Includes index.
    ISBN 0-7615-1702-2
    1. Low-fat diet—Recipes.   I. Title.
RM237.7.C7589   1998
641.5'638—dc21   98-27194
                                                                        CIP

98 99 00 01 AA 10 9 8 7 6 5 4 3 2 1

Printed in the United States of America

How to Order
Single copies may be ordered from Prima Publishing, P.O. Box 1260BK, Rocklin, CA 95677; telephone (916) 632-4400. Quantity discounts are also available. On your letterhead, include information concerning the intended use of the books and the number of books you wish to purchase.

Visit us online at www.primapublishing.com

To Alice

Contents

Acknowledgments

The work of putting this cookbook together was made easier by many people. I gratefully acknowledge the willingness of family and friends to share their skills and ideas with me.

A special thank you to Jean Smith of Tulsa.

A very special thanks to my good friend Alice Ann Williams for her neat ideas, cooking, and recipe testing. Thanks also for her writing skills and help with putting the final touches on this cookbook.

An equal amount of affectionate gratitude goes to my nephew, Greg Duckwall, for his great ideas, hard work, and enthusiastic support in everything I do.

I owe my fondest thanks to Maurice Gershon, my good friend who continues to encourage and support me.

My sincere appreciation also goes to Mary Ann Grimsley and Deidre Warren, my two wonderful caterers. Their creative cooking skills and enthusiasm made recipe testing especially fun.

I especially want to thank my good friends Rick, Rodette, and Staci Green for their encouragement, ideas, and tasting expertise.

Thanks to my sister, Marylin Nelson, for the hours she put in keeping my kitchen clean and running countless errands.*

*In Loving Memory of My Sister, Marylin Jean Nelson, 1937–1993

A large and heartfelt thank you to Steve of Steve's Sundries & Books in Tulsa. His encouragement and willingness to share invaluable advice with me is a blessing.

I will always value and appreciate the advice and encouragement from my friend and lawyer, Michael Morgan.

I am so fortunate to have Jamie Miller at Prima Publishing for my acquisitions editor. She is absolutely "The Best!" And Michelle McCormack, my project editor, has always been a sweetheart to work with.

My heartfelt thanks to my office and kitchen assistants, Trena Farmer, Erin Crabb, and Brandon Barnes. I couldn't have made it without them.

I especially want to thank Hugh and Kathy Merrill for their computer knowledge and typing skills.

Introduction

Years ago I struggled with my weight and the many
health problems that go with being obese. After I lost
100 pounds, the big challenge lay before me—keeping it
off! I chose lowfat eating because it fit my lifestyle, and I
didn't have to give up delicious foods.

Diets that require drastic changes and strict, near-
starvation guidelines just do not work! The secret to successful dieting is lifestyle change, and lowfat eating will fit
how you live.

You may be considering a lowfat diet to lose weight
or improve your health. Perhaps you are choosing to eat
lowfat foods to avoid health problems in the future. What-
ever your reason, I hope you will discover, through this
cookbook, how wonderful fat free and ultra lowfat foods
can taste. We're not talking about diet foods here—just
real food that tastes wonderful and is lowfat!

Several years ago, I opened my own weight-loss
center, guiding dieters on a lowfat eating plan. I began
creating lowfat and fat-free recipes for my dieters, and the
result was my first *Fat Free & Ultra Low Fat Recipes* cookbook. Since then, I have had the pleasure of hearing from
many of you, either through letters or phone calls, or personally at some of my seminars. My greatest joy is to hear
about the successes you have had with my recipes,

whether it is weight loss or improved health, or simply a recipe that you and your family enjoyed. The enthusiasm you have shown for my first book prompted me to write my other books *Fat Free & Ultra Lowfat Recipes, Doris' Fat-Free Homestyle Cooking,* and now this one. I hope all of them serve you well—in your kitchens and in your lives.

Sincerely,

Doris Cross

P.S. If you bought my first cookbook, you will probably notice that I have used much more fresh garlic in this one. I've decided to include more fresh garlic because of the health benefits it might provide. You may substitute garlic powder if you wish, but I personally like the taste of fresh garlic. If you've never used fresh garlic, buy yourself a garlic press and give it a try! Simply peel a clove, place it in the press, and squeeze. It's simple!

Fat-Free & Ultra Lowfat Shopping Guide

Items

Cheddar cheese from Cabot Farms in Cabot, Vermont, is the most heavenly, with only 2 grams of fat per ounce. It's wonderful to just pick up and eat a chunk; it tastes like a full-fat Cheddar cheese! This product also melts beautifully and grates nicely. To order by mail call (800) 639-3198. Ask for the 75% reduced-fat Cheddar.

Buttermist cooking spray is probably my favorite product. I use it every day. It has the same calorie and fat content as other nonstick cooking sprays, except this one tastes like real butter! Spray it on toast, bagels, English muffins, and popcorn. (Bread items taste best if lightly sprayed before toasting.) To order Buttermist with your Visa or Mastercard call me directly: (888) 743-0989. To order by mail, send a check for $19.50 for two 14-ounce cans to:

Doris' Diet Recipes
P.O. Box 549
Stillwater, OK 74076

Turkey bacon is wonderful and has all sorts of possibilities, from bacon-and-tomato sandwiches to seasoning other foods and dishes.

When buying **tortillas,** especially flour, be sure to read the label. Some have 1 or 2 grams of fat, while others have 5, 6, or 7 grams of fat. Look for fat-free tortillas also.

Some **honey mustards** are fat free and some are high in fat. Read the label and be careful of any that list soybean oil as the first or second ingredient.

Most **barbecue sauces, ketchups,** and **mustards** are fat free.

Baked Tostito's are also great with salsa and fat-free dips.

Lays Baked Potato Chips are great! In both original and BBQ flavors.

New **"Wow"** chips taste wonderful. I'm always a little careful about new products like this, but my guess is they are going to be very big.

Promise Ultra is a nonfat margarine, which will satisfy some people who crave butter. This is a spread only, and is **not** suitable for cooking or baking.

Product Brands

Reames Free frozen homestyle noodles are fat free and delicious! The new No Yolk Noodles are also very good.

Healthy Choice and **Kraft** fat-free cheeses are my favorites right now. **Borden** also has great fat-free cheese slices.

Land O' Lakes has the best fat-free sour cream, in my opinion. This should be widely available in supermarkets.

Pioneer is a fabulous brand with endless possibilities — their Low-Fat Biscuit Mix is a wonderful product. It is made in San Antonio, Texas, and is only available on a regional basis. To inquire about availability in your area, call (210) 227-1401. Pioneer also makes fat-free brown, chicken, and country gravy mixes. And just out on the market, fat-free pancake mix.

There are few brands of hot dogs that I would consider lowfat: **Healthy Choice, Hormel Light and Lean,** and **Oscar Meyer Healthy Favorites.** These have 1 or 2 grams of fat. Do not buy other hot dogs, such as those made with turkey or chicken. They are much too high in fat. **Oscar Meyer** also has a fat-free hot dog.

Campbell's has done a great job of creating some very lowfat condensed soups for casseroles and sauces. Some of my favorites include cream of mushroom, cream of chicken, cream of celery, and cream of broccoli.

Entenmann's has brought us many delicious fat-free coffee cakes, cookies, muffins, and dessert cakes. The golden pound cake makes a wonderful base for berries, making it possible to have fat-free shortcake. Just remember these desserts are not calorie free, so enjoy in moderation!

Nabisco has done great things for us with their line of **SnackWell's** cookies and crackers. They are all very good.

If you are eating a lowfat diet to lose weight, the lowfat cookies and desserts are marvelous alternatives to high-fat treats. Just remember that you cannot expect to lose weight if you eat unlimited amounts of something simply because it is fat free. Use moderation!

Tips for Successful Weight Loss

- Remember, there are two things that contribute to successful weight loss: commitment and planning.
- Have a plan and follow it exactly.
- Do not diet or lose weight for someone else—do it for yourself. You deserve it!
- Be committed! No one can do this for you—you must do it for yourself.
- Exercise daily, as permitted by your physician.
- Eat a variety of foods. Do not eat the same foods every day.
- Do not shop for groceries when you are hungry.
- Carry fruit with you so that when you get hungry, you will have the proper foods to eat.
- Have raw vegetables prepared and in the refrigerator at all times.
- When traveling, let a grocery store be your fast-food place. There are plenty of fresh fruits you can grab and eat on the way.
- Remember, the amount of fat and calories in your diet determines the amount of fat on your body. Consequently, if you eat less each day than your body burns, the result is a slimmer you.

- When eating chicken or turkey, always choose the white meat; the dark meat has more fat.
- If you're involved in a weight-loss program, have a support system to help you and to encourage you on your way to your goal; dieters who have some type of support system (spouse, counselor, etc.) lose 30% more weight than people who diet on their own.
- Seek the support you need from a diet counselor, family, and friends. Let them know how important this is to you.
- Pay attention to emotional triggers that might cause you to eat something that is not on your weight-loss plan. Go for a walk instead of giving in to the urge to eat.
- Try not to stay away from social functions because you are on a diet. Plan ahead and decide how you will handle the food that is going to be available; then go and enjoy yourself.
- Dieting is hard work! It takes effort. Make a strong commitment to eat healthily; follow your plan and then enjoy the results.
- There is no magic diet, pill, or plan to take weight off. Losing weight takes commitment and planning on your part.
- Anything worth having is worth working for—this applies to weight loss as well. Give it all you've got.

Good Luck!

Appetizers, Dips, and Breads

Gourmet Garlic Bread

Barbecue Wiener Tidbits

Creamy Horseradish Spread for Sandwiches

Sweet and Sour Chicken Rolls

Sliced Cucumbers in Sour Cream Garlic Sauce

Creamy Honey-Mustard Spread for Sandwiches

Dijon Mayonnaise Spread for Sandwiches

Cream Cheese Sandwiches on Rye Party Bread

Green Chile Queso

David's Ranch and Dill Pretzels

Garlic-Cheese Homestyle Biscuits

Garlic Butter with Fresh Basil

Crispy Veggie Rolls

Walnut-Raisin Cream Cheese

Mexican Layered Dip

Parmesan Cheese Popcorn

Sour Cream, Cheese, and Spinach Dip

Party Mix

Holiday Corn Bread Dressing

Garlic Toast

Cucumber and Garlic Cream Cheese Spread

Date Muffins

Garlic Cream Cheese Spread

Honey Mustard Bavarian Pretzels

Oriental Meatballs

Artichoke Hearts in Lemon Butter Sauce

Cream Cheese Pesto with Sun-Dried Tomatoes

Golden Waffles

Homemade Bagel Croutons

Almond Poppy Seed Muffins

Corn Bread Onion Bake

Deviled Eggs

Orange Breakfast Rolls

Cinnamon Roll-Ups

Cinnamon Pull-Aparts

Ultimate Baked Garlic

Clam Dip

Spicy Hot Bean Dip

Potato Skins Deluxe

Carrot Muffins

Orange Raisin Quick Bread

Chicken Pâté

Cherry Breakfast Danish

Banana Bread

Sweet Corn Bread

Ranch and Cheese Quick Bread

Pineapple Muffins

Gourmet Garlic Bread

---✣---

1 loaf fat-free, unsliced sourdough or French bread
$\frac{1}{2}$ cup fat-free mayonnaise
1 tablespoon fat-free plain yogurt
1 tablespoon garlic, chopped or pressed
$\frac{1}{2}$ cup fat-free Parmesan cheese or 1 cup fat-free
    Cheddar cheese

Preheat broiler

Slice bread into $\frac{1}{4}$-inch-thick slices. Place on ungreased cookie sheet.

Mix mayonnaise, yogurt, and garlic in small bowl until smooth. Spread over bread and sprinkle with Parmesan or Cheddar cheese. Broil 5 minutes or until toasted. Great with basil sprinkled on top.

Recipe makes 16 servings.

Each serving provides:

93	Calories	0.7 g	Dietary fiber
0.2 g	Fat	268 mg	Sodium
2.7 g	Protein	2 mg	Cholesterol
19.2 g	Carbohydrates		

Recipe contributed by: Jana R. Love, M.S.
Manager, Therapeutic Exercise Services
St. John Medical Center
Tulsa, Oklahoma

Barbecue Wiener Tidbits

1½ cups barbecue sauce
1 jar (12 ounces) grape jelly
8 fat-free hot dogs
1 green pepper, cut into chunks
1 medium onion, cut into chunks
1 can (15¼ ounces) pineapple chunks, drained

In large pot, combine barbecue sauce and jelly; stir with whisk over medium heat until jelly is dissolved and mixture begins to boil slightly.

Cut hot dogs into bite-sized pieces; add to barbecue sauce and simmer 5 minutes. Add green pepper and onion and simmer 5 more minutes. Add pineapple just before serving.

Recipe makes 8 servings.

Each serving provides:

231	Calories	1.6 g	Dietary fiber
0.9 g	Fat	979 mg	Sodium
6.3 g	Protein	15 mg	Cholesterol
48.5 g	Carbohydrates		

Creamy Horseradish Spread for Sandwiches

½ cup (4 ounces) Kraft fat-free cream cheese
½ cup fat-free mayonnaise
1 teaspoon prepared horseradish
Dash of garlic salt
Dash of white pepper

In small bowl, stir cream cheese by hand. Add remaining ingredients and mix thoroughly. Chill and use as needed for sandwiches, etc.

Recipe makes 8 servings. Serving size is 2 tablespoons.

Each serving provides:

27	Calories	0 g	Dietary fiber
0 g	Fat	290 mg	Sodium
2.5 g	Protein	1 mg	Cholesterol
4.1 g	Carbohydrates		

Sweet and Sour Chicken Rolls

Filling
1 pound boneless, skinless chicken breasts,
    cut into small pieces
½ teaspoon garlic salt
Pineapple juice (reserved from tidbits below)
2 teaspoons lite soy sauce
1 can (15¼ ounces) pineapple tidbits (save juice)
½ large green pepper, chopped
1 medium white onion, chopped
⅓ cup La Choy sweet and sour sauce (save remaining
    sauce in jar for dipping)

12 egg roll wrappers

Preheat oven to 350 degrees F

Add chicken pieces to skillet sprayed with nonstick
cooking spray; start to brown chicken. As chicken is
browning, add garlic salt and continue cooking until
golden brown. Add juice from pineapple and soy sauce.
Stir and simmer over medium heat until all liquid is
absorbed. Set aside to cool.

In large bowl, combine all remaining ingredients,
except sweet and sour sauce, and toss. Add chicken
and mix.

Place about ¼ cup chicken mixture in center of each egg roll wrapper. Fold and roll wrapper around filling according to package directions.

Place finished rolls on baking sheet sprayed with nonstick cooking spray, then spray tops lightly with nonstick spray. Bake for 25–30 minutes or until golden brown. Serve warm with sweet and sour sauce.

Recipe makes 12 rolls. Serving size is 2 rolls.

Each serving provides:

138	Calories	1.1 g	Dietary fiber
0.6 g	Fat	176 mg	Sodium
11.4 g	Protein	22 mg	Cholesterol
21.7 g	Carbohydrates		

Sliced Cucumbers in Sour Cream Garlic Sauce

¾ cup fat-free sour cream
¼ teaspoon seasoned salt
1 clove garlic, pressed
2 green onions, chopped
Black pepper to taste
1 large cucumber, sliced

In medium bowl, combine all ingredients except cucumber and stir until mixed. Pour mixture over sliced cucumber and chill about 1 hour before serving.

Recipe makes 4 servings.

Each serving provides:

43	Calories	0.8 g	Dietary fiber
0.1 g	Fat	124 mg	Sodium
3.6 g	Protein	0 mg	Cholesterol
7.4 g	Carbohydrates		

Creamy Honey-Mustard Spread for Sandwiches

½ cup (4 ounces) Kraft fat-free cream cheese
¼ cup Dijon mustard
⅓ cup honey

In small bowl, mix cream cheese by hand. Add remaining ingredients and stir. Chill and use as needed for sandwiches, etc.

Recipe makes 6 servings. Serving size is 2 tablespoons.

Each serving provides:

105	Calories	0 g	Dietary fiber
1 g	Fat	91 mg	Sodium
2.8 g	Protein	3 mg	Cholesterol
22.5 g	Carbohydrates		

Dijon Mayonnaise Spread for Sandwiches

1 cup fat-free mayonnaise
1 tablespoon Dijon mustard
Dash of garlic salt
Dash of black pepper

In small bowl, mix all ingredients by hand. Chill and use as needed on sandwiches, etc.

Recipe makes 8 servings. Serving size is 2 tablespoons.

Each serving provides:

26	Calories	0 g	Dietary fiber
0.1 g	Fat	452 mg	Sodium
0.1 g	Protein	0 mg	Cholesterol
6.1 g	Carbohydrates		

Cream Cheese Sandwiches on Rye Party Bread

1 can (8 ounces) crushed pineapple, very well drained
1½ cups (12 ounces) Kraft fat-free cream cheese
2 tablespoons green pepper, chopped
1 teaspoon dry onion flakes
2 teaspoons sugar
¼ teaspoon seasoned salt (optional)
1 loaf sliced rye party bread

In medium bowl, combine all ingredients except bread and stir until well mixed. Chill well, then use as spread on party rye.

Recipe makes 10 servings.

Each serving provides:

93	Calories	1.8 g	Dietary fiber
0.3 g	Fat	186 mg	Sodium
3.6 g	Protein	0 mg	Cholesterol
18.7 g	Carbohydrates		

Green Chile Queso

—❧❦—

4 slices Kraft fat-free American or Cheddar cheese
1 can (10 ounces) green chile enchilada sauce
½ cup stewed chopped tomatoes
1 can (4 ounces) chopped green chilies
2 teaspoons dry onion flakes
1 clove garlic, pressed or ¼ teaspoon garlic powder

In food processor, blend cheese and enchilada sauce until smooth. Combine with remaining ingredients and simmer in saucepan until heated. Serve warm with no-oil tortilla chips.

Note: Warm over very low heat. If heat is too high, cheese will separate and curdle.

Recipe makes 8 servings.

Each serving provides:

56	Calories	0.4 g	Dietary fiber
1.9 g	Fat	538 mg	Sodium
2.8 g	Protein	0 mg	Cholesterol
7.5 g	Carbohydrates		

David's Ranch and Dill Pretzels

1 package (18 ounces) large broken pretzels
Nonfat butter-flavored nonstick cooking spray
1 package (2 ounces) dry ranch dressing mix
½ teaspoon (approximately) garlic powder
2 teaspoons (approximately) dill weed

Preheat oven to 225 degrees F

Place broken pretzels in large bowl and spray lightly
with Buttermist. Sprinkle lightly with ranch dressing
mix, garlic powder, and dill weed. Toss and repeat
2 more times.

Pour onto baking sheet sprayed with nonstick
cooking spray and bake for 1 hour. Remove and cool.
After thoroughly cooled, store in airtight container
or resealable plastic bag.

Recipe makes 8 servings.

Each serving provides:

267	Calories	0.4 g	Dietary fiber
4.7 g	Fat	2485 mg	Sodium
8.3 g	Protein	0 mg	Cholesterol
50.6 g	Carbohydrates		

David Solomon gave me the idea for this recipe.
It's great!

Garlic-Cheese Homestyle Biscuits

2 cups Pioneer Low-Fat Biscuit Mix*
¾ cup plus 1 tablespoon evaporated skim milk
½ cup grated fat-free Cheddar cheese
Garlic salt to taste

Preheat Oven to 425 degrees F

In large bowl, combine biscuit mix, evaporated milk, and
cheese and mix well. Drop on baking sheet sprayed with
nonstick cooking spray and sprinkle tops with garlic salt.
Bake for 10–12 minutes.

Recipe makes 6 biscuits.

Each serving provides:

241	Calories	0.9 g	Dietary fiber
0.7 g	Fat	785 mg	Sodium
9.7 g	Protein	3 mg	Cholesterol
57.6 g	Carbohydrates		

---

*If you can't find Pioneer Low-Fat Biscuit Mix in your area, use
a light biscuit mix; however, this substitution will add a few grams
of fat to each serving.

Garlic Butter with Fresh Basil

2 tablespoons Molly McButter
1 tablespoon Butter Buds
¼ cup water
2 cloves garlic, pressed
Few leaves of fresh basil (optional)

Combine all ingredients in small saucepan and heat
1–2 minutes over low heat. Remove from heat
and serve.

Recipe makes 3 servings.

Each serving provides:

19	Calories	0 g	Dietary fiber
0.1 g	Fat	467 mg	Sodium
0.1 g	Protein	0 mg	Cholesterol
4.1 g	Carbohydrates		

Crispy Veggie Rolls

Filling
1 package (10 ounces) frozen corn, thawed
1 package (10 ounces) frozen chopped broccoli, thawed
1 medium onion, chopped
4 tablespoons Kraft fat-free cream cheese
$\frac{1}{3}$ cup fat-free Parmesan cheese
1 tablespoon Molly McButter
$\frac{1}{2}$ teaspoon seasoned salt
Dash of garlic salt
Black pepper to taste

14 egg roll wrappers

Dipping Sauce
$\frac{1}{2}$ cup (4 ounces) Kraft fat-free cream cheese
1 cup fat-free sour cream
1 package (2 ounces) dry ranch dressing mix

Preheat oven to 350 degrees F

In large bowl, combine filling ingredients and stir with spoon until well blended. Place about $\frac{1}{4}$ cup filling in center of each egg roll wrapper. Fold wrapper according to package directions.

Place finished rolls on baking sheet sprayed with nonstick cooking spray, then spray tops lightly with nonstick spray. Bake for 25–30 minutes or until golden brown.

Prepare dipping sauce while rolls are baking. In food processor, combine all ingredients and process until smooth. Refrigerate until ready to serve with veggie rolls.

Recipe makes 7 servings. Serving size is 2 rolls.

Each serving provides:

347	Calories	4 g	Dietary fiber
0.3 g	Fat	2084 mg	Sodium
19.3 g	Protein	6 mg	Cholesterol
69.6 g	Carbohydrates		

Walnut-Raisin Cream Cheese

1½ cups (12 ounces) Kraft fat-free cream cheese
⅓ cup raisins
2 tablespoons black walnut pieces, chopped fine
⅓ cup brown sugar

In medium bowl, combine ingredients and mix with electric mixer until sugar is dissolved.

This spreads better if refrigerated for a few hours after mixing.

Recipe makes 18 servings. Serving size is 2 tablespoons.

Each serving provides:

47	Calories	0.2 g	Dietary fiber
0.5 g	Fat	93 mg	Sodium
3 g	Protein	3 mg	Cholesterol
7.8 g	Carbohydrates		

Mexican Layered Dip

---

1 pound ground turkey breast or chicken breast
1 package (1¼ ounces) dry taco seasoning
½ cup water
1 can (16 ounces) fat-free refried beans
1 can (4 ounces) chopped green chilies
1 small onion, chopped
1 cup fat-free sour cream
½ cup fat-free cheese, grated
1 large tomato, chopped (optional)

Brown meat in skillet sprayed with nonstick cooking spray. Add taco seasoning and water. Simmer and stir until all water is cooked away. Set aside to cool.

Spread refried beans evenly over bottom of 8- or 9-inch round or square baking dish. Layer with meat, green chilies, onion, and sour cream. Top with grated cheese and tomatoes. Chill and serve with no-oil tortilla chips.

Recipe makes 8 servings.

Each serving provides:

185	Calories	4.4 g	Dietary fiber
1.8 g	Fat	706 mg	Sodium
22.4 g	Protein	35 mg	Cholesterol
19.7 g	Carbohydrates		

Parmesan Cheese Popcorn

8–10 cups air-popped popcorn
Buttermist*
⅓ cup fat-free Parmesan cheese
Salt to taste (optional)

Lightly spray popped corn with Buttermist and immediately sprinkle on about 1 tablespoon Parmesan. Toss popcorn, add salt to taste, and repeat process.

Blackened Parmesan Cheese Popcorn
Follow recipe above and add 1–2 teaspoons blackened or Cajun spices.**

Recipe makes about 10 servings. One serving equals 1 cup.

Each serving provides:

43	Calories	0.4 g	Dietary fiber
0.7 g	Fat	35 mg	Sodium
1.3 g	Protein	2 mg	Cholesterol
7.6 g	Carbohydrates		

---

*Any butter-flavored cooking spray will work; however, I prefer the taste of Buttermist because it tastes like real butter.
**This will increase sodium level to 115 mg. All other nutrition information remains the same

Sour Cream, Cheese, and Spinach Dip

1 cup fat-free sour cream
7 slices Kraft fat-free American cheese
½ cup fat-free chicken broth
¼–½ teaspoon seasoned salt
½ cup frozen chopped spinach, thawed,
    drained thoroughly
2–3 tablespoons green chilies, chopped
2 teaspoons dry onion flakes

In food processor, mix sour cream, cheese, chicken broth, and seasoned salt. Pour into small saucepan or very small Crock Pot and add spinach, green chilies, and onion flakes. Warm and serve.

Recipe makes 4 servings.

	Each serving provides:		
113	Calories	1 g	Dietary fiber
0.3 g	Fat	853 mg	Sodium
14.2 g	Protein	0 mg	Cholesterol
15.2 g	Carbohydrates		

Party Mix

Note: You will need a small, clean spray bottle.

3 cups Rice Chex
3 cups Corn Chex
3 cups Cheerios
3 cups fat-free pretzels
Worcestershire sauce
Buttermist*
Seasoned salt
Garlic powder
Onion powder (optional)

Preheat oven to 200 degrees F

In large pan, combine dry cereals and pretzels. Pour Worcestershire in small spray bottle. Lightly spray top of cereal mixture with Worcestershire, then with Buttermist.

---

*Any butter-flavored cooking spray will work; however, I prefer the taste of Buttermist because it tastes like real butter.

Lightly sprinkle mixture with seasoned salt, garlic powder, and onion powder. Stir and repeat this process several times. Be careful not to use too much seasoned salt, as it is very salty.

Bake for 1½ hours, stirring every 30 minutes. Allow to cool and store in air-tight container.

Recipe makes 6 servings.

Each serving provides:

216	Calories	2 g	Dietary fiber
2 g	Fat	608 mg	Sodium
4.6 g	Protein	0 mg	Cholesterol
46.2 g	Carbohydrates		

Holiday Corn Bread Dressing

Dry 7 slices of lowfat bread before preparing dressing.

Corn Bread for Dressing
1¼ cups yellow cornmeal
⅓ cup sugar
¼ teaspoon (heaping) salt
¼ teaspoon baking soda
2 teaspoons baking powder
1 egg white, slightly beaten
1¼ cups lowfat buttermilk

Remaining Ingredients for Dressing
1 medium onion, chopped
4 stalks celery, chopped
2 egg whites, slightly beaten
2 cans (14 ounces each) low-sodium, fat-free
    chicken broth
1½ teaspoons rubbed sage
Salt and black pepper to taste

Preheat oven to 400 degrees F

Combine dry corn bread ingredients and mix. Add egg white and buttermilk and mix. Pour into small square or round pan sprayed with nonstick cooking spray. Bake for 25–30 minutes. Cool and break into chunks.

Reduce oven heat to 350 degrees F. In a skillet sprayed with nonstick cooking spray, simmer onion and celery until tender; set aside.

In large bowl, break up pieces of dried bread and corn bread and mix. Add onion, celery, egg whites, chicken broth, and sage. Mix thoroughly. Add salt and pepper. Pour into 11 × 7 inch baking dish sprayed with nonstick cooking spray. Bake for 50–60 minutes or until golden brown on edges and top.

Recipe makes 8 servings.

	Each serving provides:		
209	Calories	2.4 g	Dietary fiber
1.6 g	Fat	487 mg	Sodium
7.7 g	Protein	1 mg	Cholesterol
41.2 g	Carbohydrates		

Garlic Toast

1 loaf lowfat or fat-free sourdough bread, sliced
Nonfat butter-flavored nonstick cooking spray
Garlic salt

Preheat oven to 375 degrees F

Place slices of bread on cookie sheet sprayed with cooking spray. Spray top of bread lightly with cooking spray. Sprinkle lightly with garlic salt. Bake for 7–10 minutes or until golden brown.

Parmesan Cheese Toast
Same as above, adding fat-free Parmesan cheese.

Ranch Parmesan Cheese Toast
Same as above, omitting garlic salt and adding garlic powder and dry ranch dressing mix.

Recipe makes 10 servings (from 1-pound loaf).

Each serving provides:

124	Calories	1 g	Dietary fiber
0.5 g	Fat	224 mg	Sodium
3.4 g	Protein	0 mg	Cholesterol
25.4 g	Carbohydrates		

Cucumber and Garlic Cream Cheese Spread

1 cup (8 ounces) fat-free cream cheese
2 tablespoons cucumber, finely chopped
1 clove garlic, pressed
2 teaspoons dry onion flakes
$\frac{1}{8}$–$\frac{1}{4}$ teaspoon seasoned salt

In small bowl, combine all ingredients and mix well.
Chill and serve on bagels or English muffins.

Recipe makes 8 servings.

Each serving provides:

30	Calories	0.1 g	Dietary fiber
0 g	Fat	166 mg	Sodium
4.1 g	Protein	5 mg	Cholesterol
3.2 g	Carbohydrates		

Date Muffins

—⧜—

1 cup all-purpose flour
$\frac{1}{4}$ cup sugar
$1\frac{1}{2}$ teaspoons baking powder
$\frac{1}{4}$ teaspoon baking soda
1 teaspoon Molly McButter
$\frac{1}{4}$ cup fat-free liquid egg product
1 teaspoon vanilla
$\frac{1}{2}$ cup plus 2 tablespoons lowfat buttermilk
$\frac{1}{4}$ cup fat-free Eagle Brand milk
$\frac{1}{2}$ cup chopped dates
$\frac{1}{2}$ cup applesauce

Preheat oven to 375 degrees F

In large bowl, combine flour, sugar, baking powder, soda, and Molly McButter. Mix thoroughly. Add all remaining ingredients and mix.

Spray 12-hole muffin tin with nonstick cooking spray. **Do not use paper liners.** Fill 9 holes $\frac{3}{4}$ full of batter. Bake for 15–20 minutes.

Recipe makes 9 servings.

Each serving provides:

147	Calories	1 g	Dietary fiber
0.4 g	Fat	186 mg	Sodium
3.5 g	Protein	2 mg	Cholesterol
33.2 g	Carbohydrates		

Garlic Cream Cheese Spread

---

1 tub (8 ounces) fat-free cream cheese
2 cloves garlic, pressed
1 teaspoon dried or fresh chives, chopped
1 teaspoon dry onion flakes
1 tablespoon minced fresh parsley
¼ cup Sargento light grated Cheddar cheese
Garlic salt and black pepper to taste

In medium bowl, cream fat-free cream cheese with
electric mixer until smooth. Add all remaining ingredients and mix. Chill for an hour or more before serving.
Great served on crackers for a party.

Recipe makes 4 servings.

Each serving provides:

71	Calories	0.1 g	Dietary fiber
1.1 g	Fat	321 mg	Sodium
10.2 g	Protein	12 mg	Cholesterol
5.1 g	Carbohydrates		

Honey Mustard
Bavarian Pretzels

1 package (18 ounces) large broken pretzels or
    1 box large Bavarian pretzels, broken into chunks
¾ cup sweet mustard or honey mustard (find one that
    does not contain oil)
2 teaspoons dry Hidden Valley Ranch Honey Dijon
    dressing mix
Nonfat butter-flavored nonstick cooking spray

Preheat oven to 250 degrees F

Pour pretzels into large bowl and drizzle half the
mustard over pretzels. Stir with large spoon and
drizzle remaining mustard over pretzels. Stir again to
distribute mustard.

Sprinkle with small amount of dry dressing mix
and toss. Repeat until the remaining dressing mix is
used. Spray lightly with cooking spray and toss. Repeat
two more times.

Pour pretzels on baking sheet sprayed with
Buttermist or nonstick cooking spray and bake for
1 hour, stirring every 20 minutes. Remove and cool.

Recipe makes 10 servings.

Each serving provides:

260	Calories	0.3 g	Dietary fiber
5.6 g	Fat	1422 mg	Sodium
5.8 g	Protein	0 mg	Cholesterol
50.3 g	Carbohydrates		

Oriental Meatballs

Meatballs
1 pound ground chicken breast or turkey breast
1 can (8 ounces) crushed pineapple, drained
¾ cup cooked rice
1 egg white, slightly beaten
1 carrot, grated
⅓ cup bell pepper, chopped
1 tablespoon lite soy sauce
2 teaspoons dry onion flakes

Sweet and Sour Sauce
1 jar (18 ounces) sweet orange marmalade
2 teaspoons lite soy sauce
1 tablespoon vinegar

Preheat oven to 375 degrees F

Combine all ingredients for meatballs and form into
1 inch balls. Place on baking sheet sprayed with nonstick
cooking spray and bake for 20 minutes or until brown.

In small bowl, combine all ingredients for sauce.
Use as dip for meatballs or spoon over top when served.

Recipe makes 8 servings.

Each serving provides:

336	Calories	0.9 g	Dietary fiber
0.8 g	Fat	176 mg	Sodium
15.1 g	Protein	34 mg	Cholesterol
60.3 g	Carbohydrates		

Artichoke Hearts in Lemon Butter Sauce

1 can (14 ounces) artichoke hearts, packed in water
Juice from 1 lemon
2 cloves garlic, pressed
2 teaspoons Molly McButter
⅓ pound lite ham, shaved
¼ cup fat-free Parmesan cheese

Preheat oven to 350 degrees F

Pour water off artichoke hearts and turn each upside down on paper towel to drain.

In small saucepan, combine lemon juice, garlic, and Molly McButter. Warm slightly and stir; set aside.

Choose small baking dish in which artichoke hearts will fit closely, standing up; spray baking dish with non-stick cooking spray. Cut ham into long strips and wrap each artichoke heart with 1 strip of ham.

Place each wrapped artichoke standing up in baking dish. When all are wrapped and placed in dish, pour lemon juice mixture over top, filling each heart. Sprinkle with Parmesan and bake for 15–20 minutes. Serve warm.

Recipe makes 4 servings.

Each serving provides:

93	Calories	0.8 g	Dietary fiber
1.2 g	Fat	665 mg	Sodium
8.3 g	Protein	21 mg	Cholesterol
11.2 g	Carbohydrates		

Cream Cheese Pesto with Sun-Dried Tomatoes

Cream Cheese Layer
1½ cups (12 ounces) Kraft fat-free cream cheese
1 clove garlic, pressed
1 teaspoon dry onion flakes

Tomato Layer
½ cup sun-dried tomatoes
2 cups boiling water

Pesto Layer
½ cup fat-free Parmesan cheese
2½ teaspoons Molly McButter
½ cup fresh sweet basil leaves, chopped
      (measure before chopping)
2 tablespoons fat-free chicken broth
1 clove garlic, pressed
Garlic salt

Combine cream cheese layer ingredients and mix thoroughly.

In small saucepan, cook tomatoes in boiling water 3–4 minutes. Set aside to cool; then drain. Process in food processor into small pieces; pour into small bowl and set aside.

Combine ingredients for pesto layer and stir until thoroughly mixed.

In small bowl, spread thin layer of cream cheese mixture. Use all the tomato mixture for next layer. Gently drop and spread another layer of cream cheese mixture; then gently spread pesto over top. Add remaining cream cheese mixture for top layer and lightly sprinkle with garlic salt. Chill and serve with toast, bagels, crackers, or bagel chips.

Recipe makes 6 servings.

Each serving provides:

115	Calories	1.4 g	Dietary fiber
0.2 g	Fat	463 mg	Sodium
10.9 g	Protein	13 mg	Cholesterol
16 g	Carbohydrates		

Golden Waffles

---&—

1½ cups fat-free liquid egg product
1 cup fat-free cottage cheese
½ cup flour
¼ cup skim milk
1 teaspoon Molly McButter
1 tablespoon sugar
¼ teaspoon salt

Combine all ingredients in food processor and blend
1 minute. Cook on waffle iron sprayed with nonstick
cooking spray according to waffle iron directions.

Recipe makes 6 servings.

Each serving provides:

105	Calories	0.3 g	Dietary fiber
0.3 g	Fat	347 mg	Sodium
12.4 g	Protein	3 mg	Cholesterol
12.9 g	Carbohydrates		

Homemade Bagel Croutons

—— ✣ ——

2 bagels
Nonfat butter-flavored nonstick cooking spray
Suggested various seasonings to sprinkle on:
    Garlic powder
    Garlic salt
    Onion powder
    Dry ranch dressing mix
    Dill weed
    Fat-free Parmesan cheese

Preheat oven to 375 degrees F

Cut bagels into small pieces and spread on baking
sheet sprayed with nonstick cooking spray. Lightly
spray bagel pieces with cooking spray. Sprinkle on any
desired seasoning.
    Bake for 5–12 minutes or until lightly browned.
Remove from oven and cool. Use in soups or salads.

Recipe makes 4 servings.

Each serving provides:

165	Calories	1.2 g	Dietary fiber
1.6 g	Fat	514 mg	Sodium
6 g	Protein	0 mg	Cholesterol
30.9 g	Carbohydrates		

Almond Poppy Seed Muffins

—❧⦃—

1 cup all-purpose flour
1½ teaspoons baking powder
⅓ cup sugar
1 teaspoon Molly McButter
¼ teaspoon baking soda
1 teaspoon poppy seeds
1 teaspoon vanilla
½ cup plus 2 tablespoons lowfat buttermilk
¼ cup fat-free Eagle Brand sweetened condensed milk
¼ cup fat-free liquid egg product
½ teaspoon almond extract
⅓ cup applesauce

Preheat oven to 375 degrees F

In large bowl combine flour, baking powder, sugar, Molly McButter, baking soda, and poppy seeds and mix well. Add all remaining ingredients and stir.

Spray 12-hole muffin tin with nonstick cooking spray. **Do not use paper liners.** Fill 9 of the muffin cups ¾ full with batter. Bake for 15–20 minutes.

Recipe makes 9 servings.

Each serving provides:

123	Calories	0.5 g	Dietary fiber
0.5 g	Fat	186 mg	Sodium
3.4 g	Protein	2 mg	Cholesterol
26.2 g	Carbohydrates		

Corn Bread Onion Bake

Onion Mixture
3 large sweet onions, sliced
1 teaspoon garlic salt
¼ teaspoon black pepper
1 cup (8 ounces) Kraft fat-free cream cheese

Corn Bread
2½ cups lowfat buttermilk
½ cup sugar
½ teaspoon salt
2 egg whites
2½ cups cornmeal
½ teaspoon baking soda
1 tablespoon baking powder
1 cup shredded fat-free American cheese

Preheat oven to 400 degrees F

In large skillet sprayed with nonstick cooking spray, brown and simmer onions until slightly limp; season with garlic salt while browning. Remove from heat and add pepper and cream cheese; set aside.

In large bowl, combine buttermilk, sugar, salt, and egg whites and mix with electric mixer. In another bowl, combine cornmeal, baking soda, and baking powder and mix thoroughly. Add to buttermilk mixture and mix. Fold in cheese.

Spread half the onion mixture in large casserole sprayed with nonstick cooking spray. Pour half the corn bread batter over onions. Repeat layers. Bake for 30–35 minutes.

Recipe makes 12 servings.

Each serving provides:

223	Calories	3 g	Dietary fiber
1.1 g	Fat	649 mg	Sodium
11.4 g	Protein	7 mg	Cholesterol
42 g	Carbohydrates		

Deviled Eggs

—✦—

5 hard-boiled eggs
1 cup fat-free liquid egg product
3 tablespoons fat-free Miracle Whip
¼ teaspoon horseradish
½ teaspoon Grey Poupon mustard
½ teaspoon vinegar
⅛ teaspoon salt (optional)
Black pepper to taste
Paprika

Cut hard-boiled eggs in half horizontally and discard yolks. Chill egg white halves while preparing filling.

In skillet sprayed with nonstick cooking spray, scramble liquid egg product until done; set aside to cool.

Add scrambled eggs and all remaining ingredients except paprika to food processor and process until smooth. Fill egg white halves with mixture and sprinkle tops with paprika.

Note: If you prefer a sweeter taste, use less mustard and add 1–2 tablespoons sweet pickle relish.

Recipe makes 10 deviled eggs.

Each serving provides:

28	Calories	0 g	Dietary fiber
0.1 g	Fat	150 mg	Sodium
4.2 g	Protein	0 mg	Cholesterol
2.2 g	Carbohydrates		

Orange Breakfast Rolls

Rolls
1 can (6 ounces) frozen orange juice concentrate, thawed
Grated peel from ½ orange
1 can (7½ ounces) refrigerated biscuits (find one with
    1 gram of fat per biscuit)
½ teaspoon Molly McButter
1 tablespoon sugar

Icing
¾ cup powdered sugar
¼ cup (2 ounces) Kraft fat-free cream cheese
1 tablespoon orange juice concentrate
Grated peel from ½ orange
½ teaspoon Molly McButter

Preheat oven to 350 degrees F

Save 1 tablespoon orange juice concentrate for icing.
Mix remaining concentrate with grated orange peel.
Dip biscuits in concentrate and then place in square or
round baking dish sprayed with nonstick cooking
spray. Sprinkle tops with Molly McButter and sugar.
Bake for 30 minutes. Remove from oven.

Combine all icing ingredients and mix well. Pour
over hot rolls.

Recipe makes 8 servings.

Each serving provides:

174	Calories	0.3 g	Dietary fiber
1.2 g	Fat	423 mg	Sodium
4.5 g	Protein	2 mg	Cholesterol
37.1 g	Carbohydrates		

Cinnamon Roll-Ups

Filling
3/4 cup applesauce
1/2 cup brown sugar
1/2 teaspoon cinnamon
2 teaspoons Molly McButter
Pinch of ground cloves

Topping
1/4 cup sugar
1/4 teaspoon cinnamon

8 egg roll wrappers

Preheat oven to 375 degrees F

In small bowl, combine applesauce, brown sugar,
1/2 teaspoon cinnamon, Molly McButter, and ground
cloves. In another small bowl, combine topping
ingredients.

Place 1 egg roll wrapper on a plate and spoon about
1 1/2 tablespoons filling over surface of wrapper. Start at
one corner and roll up like a pencil, rolling on the diagonal. Finished roll will be about the size of a cigar.

Place rolls on a baking sheet sprayed with nonstick cooking spray. Lightly spray tops with nonstick spray and sprinkle with topping. Bake for 15–18 minutes or until golden brown.

Recipe makes 8 servings.

Each serving provides:

151	Calories	0.8 g	Dietary fiber
0 g	Fat	78 mg	Sodium
2 g	Protein	0 mg	Cholesterol
36.9 g	Carbohydrates		

Cinnamon Pull-Aparts

Cinnamon Paste
1 cup dark brown sugar
1 cup applesauce
2 teaspoons cinnamon
Pinch of ground cloves

Sprinkle Mixture
½ cup sugar
½ teaspoon cinnamon

3 cans (7½ ounces each) refrigerated biscuits
　　(use fat free or 1 gram fat per biscuit)
2–3 tablespoons Molly McButter

Preheat oven to 350 degrees F

In small bowl, combine ingredients for cinnamon paste
and mix. In another small bowl, combine ingredients for
sprinkle mixture.

Spray Bundt pan with nonstick cooking spray and sprinkle bottom with a little sprinkle mixture. Cut biscuits in half, dip in cinnamon paste, and cover bottom of pan with one layer. Sprinkle with a little sprinkle mixture and Molly McButter and repeat until all biscuits are used. Bake for 30–40 minutes. Serve warm.

Recipe makes 10 servings.

Each serving provides:

331	Calories	0.9 g	Dietary fiber
2.9 g	Fat	914 mg	Sodium
4.3 g	Protein	0 mg	Cholesterol
73.6 g	Carbohydrates		

Ultimate Baked Garlic

———✦———

2 large full heads of garlic
2 tablespoons white cooking wine
1 tablespoon Molly McButter
½ cup fat-free chicken broth
Garlic salt and black pepper to taste

Preheat oven to 375 degrees F

Cut across the top of each head of garlic to remove about ⅓ of the top. This will expose open cloves of garlic. Place in small baking dish.

Mix together cooking wine, Molly McButter, and chicken broth. Pour mixture over garlic heads. Sprinkle with garlic salt and pepper. Cover and bake 35–40 minutes or until garlic cloves are tender.

I love this spread on focaccia.

Recipe makes 4 servings.

Each serving provides:

51	Calories	0.6 g	Dietary fiber
0.2 g	Fat	298 mg	Sodium
2.1 g	Protein	0 mg	Cholesterol
10.9 g	Carbohydrates		

Clam Dip

1 can (6 ounces) minced clams, drained
1½ cups (12 ounces) Kraft fat-free cream cheese
⅓ cup fat-free sour cream
5–6 drops Tabasco sauce
2 teaspoons dry onion flakes
¼ teaspoon garlic powder
½ teaspoon seasoned salt (optional)
Dash of black pepper

Combine all ingredients and stir until thoroughly mixed.
Chill and serve. Good with lowfat or fat-free crackers
or pretzels.

Recipe makes 6 servings.

Each serving provides:

83	Calories	0.2 g	Dietary fiber
0.3 g	Fat	294 mg	Sodium
12.3 g	Protein	18 mg	Cholesterol
7.5 g	Carbohydrates		

Spicy Hot Bean Dip

———✧———

1 can (16 ounces) fat-free refried beans
3 green onions, chopped
2 tablespoons chopped green chilies
½ cup fat-free sour cream
½ cup shredded fat-free Cheddar cheese
2 teaspoons dry taco seasoning
Sliced jalapeños (optional)

Preheat oven to 350 degrees F

Combine all ingredients except jalapeños and mix
thoroughly. Pour into small casserole sprayed with
nonstick cooking spray and top with jalapeños. Warm
for 20–25 minutes. Serve with no-oil tortilla chips.

Recipe makes 6 servings.

Each serving provides:

115	Calories	4.9 g	Dietary fiber
0.1 g	Fat	607 mg	Sodium
9.3 g	Protein	2 mg	Cholesterol
22.7 g	Carbohydrates		

Potato Skins Deluxe

4 medium baking potatoes
1 cup fat-free sour cream
4 green onions, chopped
4 slices Mr. Turkey Maple Smoked turkey bacon
    (cooked and crushed)
½ cup Sargento light grated Cheddar cheese

Preheat oven to 400 degrees F

Bake potatoes about 1 hour at 400 degrees. Remove
from oven and allow to cool before handling. Slice each
potato in half lengthwise and scoop out some of the
center of each potato half to make room for filling.
    Spray baking sheet with nonstick cooking spray.
Fill each potato half with 1 tablespoon fat-free sour
cream, 1–2 teaspoons chopped green onions, and ½ slice
crumbled turkey bacon. Sprinkle a little grated cheese
on top. Place potato halves on baking sheet and heat at
400 degrees for 10–12 minutes.

Recipe makes 8 servings.

Each serving provides:

134	Calories	2.1 g	Dietary fiber
2.5 g	Fat	162 mg	Sodium
6.2 g	Protein	8 mg	Cholesterol
22.7 g	Carbohydrates		

Carrot Muffins

—❦—

1 cup all-purpose flour
½ cup sugar
1½ teaspoons baking powder
¼ teaspoon baking soda
½ teaspoon cinnamon
⅛ teaspoon ground cloves
½ cup finely grated carrots (not the pre-grated kind)
2 tablespoons chopped raisins
¼ cup fat-free liquid egg product
1 teaspoon vanilla
1 teaspoon Molly McButter
½ cup lowfat buttermilk
¼ cup Eagle Brand fat-free sweetened and
    condensed milk

Preheat oven to 375 degrees F

In large bowl combine flour, sugar, baking powder, baking soda, cinnamon, and cloves. Mix thoroughly. Add all remaining ingredients and mix well.

Spray 12-muffin tin with nonstick cooking spray. **Do not use paper liners.** Fill 9 cups ¾ full of batter. Bake for 20–25 minutes.

Recipe makes 9 servings.

Each serving provides:

133	Calories	0.7 g	Dietary fiber
0.3 g	Fat	185 mg	Sodium
3.3 g	Protein	2 mg	Cholesterol
29.5 g	Carbohydrates		

Orange Raisin Quick Bread

———✦———

1½ cups flour
1 teaspoon baking soda
2 teaspoons baking powder
¾ cup sugar
1 tablespoon Molly McButter
⅓ cup fat-free liquid egg product
1¼ cups applesauce
Juice and grated peel from 1 orange
¾ cup raisins
1½ cups bran cereal

Preheat oven to 325 degrees F

In large bowl, sift together flour, baking soda, baking powder, sugar, and Molly McButter.

In another bowl, combine egg product, applesauce, orange juice, and orange peel and mix with electric mixer. Stir in raisins and cereal.

Gradually add flour mixture to egg mixture and mix thoroughly. Pour into loaf pan sprayed with nonstick cooking spray and bake for 50–55 minutes.

Recipe makes 10 servings.

Each serving provides:

228	Calories	5 g	Dietary fiber
0.6 g	Fat	356 mg	Sodium
4.8 g	Protein	0 mg	Cholesterol
56.2 g	Carbohydrates		

Chicken Pâté

———⚬⚭———

4 boneless, skinless chicken breasts, cooked
1 egg white, hard-boiled and chopped (discard yolk)
1 small onion, chopped
1½ cups (6 ounces) fresh mushrooms, sliced and sautéed
½ cup (4 ounces) Kraft fat-free cream cheese
1 teaspoon garlic salt
¼ teaspoon black pepper

Cut chicken breasts into pieces and shred. Add remaining ingredients and mix thoroughly. Chill and serve.

Recipe makes 8 servings.

Each serving provides:

98	Calories	0.5 g	Dietary fiber
1.6 g	Fat	361 mg	Sodium
16.3 g	Protein	39 mg	Cholesterol
3.5 g	Carbohydrates		

Cherry Breakfast Danish

⅓ cup fat-free cottage cheese
2 tablespoons sugar
¼ teaspoon vanilla extract
1 raisin English muffin, halved and lightly toasted
2 tablespoons cherry preserves

In small bowl, combine cottage cheese, sugar, and vanilla. Spoon over English muffin halves and top with preserves. Place under broiler until warm.

Recipe makes 1 serving.

Each serving provides:

417	Calories	5.1 g	Dietary fiber
1.4 g	Fat	702 mg	Sodium
15.7 g	Protein	7 mg	Cholesterol
87.2 g	Carbohydrates		

Banana Bread

2 cups flour
1¼ cups sugar
1 teaspoon baking soda
1 tablespoon Molly McButter
⅓ cup light corn syrup
½ cup applesauce
½ cup fat-free liquid egg product
4 ripe bananas
1 teaspoon vanilla extract

Preheat oven to 350 degrees F

Combine all ingredients in large bowl and mix well.
Bake in loaf pan sprayed with nonstick cooking spray
for 50–60 minutes.

Recipe makes 10 servings.

Each serving provides:

271	Calories	1.9 g	Dietary fiber
0.5 g	Fat	214 mg	Sodium
4.3 g	Protein	0 mg	Cholesterol
64.8 g	Carbohydrates		

Sweet Corn Bread

———— ❦ ————

⅓ cup fat-free liquid egg product
1 cup evaporated skim milk
½ cup brown sugar
2 teaspoons Molly McButter
1 teaspoon salt
1¼ cups Pioneer Low-Fat Biscuit Mix*
¾ cup cornmeal

Preheat oven to 400 degrees F

In large bowl, combine egg product, evaporated milk, and brown sugar. Add Molly McButter and salt and mix thoroughly. Add biscuit mix and cornmeal and stir. Bake in 9-inch square baking dish sprayed with nonstick cooking spray for 20–25 minutes or until golden brown.

Recipe makes 9 servings.

Each serving provides:

201	Calories	1 g	Dietary fiber
5 g	Fat	615 mg	Sodium
5.6 g	Protein	1 mg	Cholesterol
47 g	Carbohydrates		

---

*If you can't find Pioneer Low-Fat Biscuit Mix in your area, use a light biscuit mix; however, this substitution will add a few grams of fat to each serving.

Ranch and Cheese
Quick Bread

2 cups all-purpose flour
4 teaspoons baking powder
1 package (1 ounce) dry ranch dressing mix
¾ cup 1 percent cottage cheese
¾ cup skim milk
¼ cup fat-free liquid egg product
¼ teaspoon dill weed
1 teaspoon Molly McButter
1 tablespoon dry onion flakes
½ cup Sargento light grated Cheddar cheese

Preheat oven to 375 degrees F

In medium bowl, combine flour, baking powder, and dry ranch dressing mix.

In another bowl, stir together cottage cheese, milk, egg product, dill weed, Molly McButter, onion flakes, and grated Cheddar cheese.

Stir together these two mixtures and mix thoroughly. Spray loaf pan with nonstick cooking spray. Pour in bread mixture and bake for 50–55 minutes.

Recipe makes 8 servings.

Each serving provides:

170	Calories	0.9 g	Dietary fiber
1.7 g	Fat	1142 mg	Sodium
10.4 g	Protein	4 mg	Cholesterol
28.2 g	Carbohydrates		

Pineapple Muffins

———— ✣ ————

1 cup all-purpose flour
1½ teaspoons baking powder
1½ teaspoons Molly McButter
⅓ cup sugar
¼ teaspoon baking soda
1 can (8 ounces) crushed pineapple (use juice)
1½ teaspoons vanilla
¼ cup low-fat buttermilk
¼ cup fat-free liquid egg product

Preheat oven to 375 degrees F

In large bowl, combine flour, baking powder, Molly
McButter, sugar, and baking soda and mix well. Add all
remaining ingredients and stir.
    Spray 12-cup muffin tin with nonstick cooking
spray. **Do not use paper liners.** Fill 9 of the cups ¾ full.
Bake for 15–20 minutes.

Recipe makes 9 servings.

Each serving provides:

103	Calories	0.6 g	Dietary fiber
0.2 g	Fat	178 mg	Sodium
2.4 g	Protein	0 mg	Cholesterol
22.8 g	Carbohydrates		

Soups, Salads, and Vegetables

Fancy Corn

Tortilla Soup

Creamy Grapefruit–Mandarin Orange Salad

Spaghetti Salad I

Mushroom and Beef Stew

Cajun Bean Soup

Pimiento Chicken Salad

Buttermilk Coleslaw

French Onion Soup

Italian Pasta Soup

Sweet and Sour Chicken Salad

Taco Chicken Salad

Summer Pasta Salad

Fruit Salad Deluxe

Creamy Southwest Soup

Creamy Potatoes

Chicken Salad Deluxe

No-Oil Tabouli

Spinach Cheese Bake

Peaches and Cream Gelatin Salad

Green Chile–Artichoke Bake

Broccoli and Cheese Soup
Salmon Pasta Salad
Corn Chip Potato Salad
Creamy Oven Hash Browns
Fancy Mashed Potatoes
Old-Fashioned Baked Beans
Sweet Potato French Fries
Black-Eyed Pea and Corn Salad
Bean Salad
Stuffed Tomatoes
Julie's Potatoes
Cajun Seafood Salad
Layered Pea Salad
Eggplant Parmesan
Seafood Rice Salad
Festive Taco Corn
Wilted Lettuce Salad
Spaghetti Salad II
Oven-Fried Okra

Fancy Corn

1 package (10 ounces) frozen corn
¾ cup (6 ounces) Kraft fat-free cream cheese
2 teaspoons dry onion flakes
¼ teaspoon garlic salt
2 teaspoons Molly McButter
Black pepper to taste

Cook corn according to package directions and drain.
Add remaining ingredients and stir over low heat
1–2 minutes. Serve.

Recipe makes 4 servings.

Each serving provides:

98	Calories	1.7 g	Dietary fiber
0.3 g	Fat	414 mg	Sodium
8 g	Protein	7 mg	Cholesterol
17.7 g	Carbohydrates		

Tortilla Soup

2 boneless, skinless chicken breasts (8 ounces total),
    cut into small pieces
1 medium onion, chopped
1 stalk celery, chopped
2 cans (14 ounces each) fat-free chicken broth
1 can (14½ ounces) stewed, chopped tomatoes
1 clove garlic, pressed
1 can (4 ounces) chopped green chilies
½ package (1¼ ounces) dry taco seasoning
½ cup fat-free sour cream
6 corn tortillas, cut into 1 inch squares

Brown chicken pieces in large pot sprayed with nonstick
cooking spray. Add onion and celery and continue to
brown. Add all remaining ingredients except sour cream
and tortillas and simmer 15 minutes.

   Add sour cream and simmer 1–2 minutes. Add
tortillas and simmer 1–2 minutes. Serve.

Recipe makes 6 servings.

Each serving provides:

200	Calories	4.4 g	Dietary fiber
1.5 g	Fat	1292 mg	Sodium
15.4 g	Protein	22 mg	Cholesterol
32.3 g	Carbohydrates		

Creamy Grapefruit–
Mandarin Orange Salad

1 can (16 ounces) grapefruit sections, drained
1 can (11 ounces) mandarin oranges, drained
½ cup (4 ounces) Kraft fat-free cream cheese
2 tablespoons sugar
½ teaspoon grated lemon peel

Combine drained fruit. In small bowl, combine remaining ingredients and stir until sugar is dissolved. Pour over fruit and toss. Chill and serve on a lettuce leaf.

Recipe makes 4 servings.

Each serving provides:

113	Calories	0.7 g	Dietary fiber
0.1 g	Fat	139 mg	Sodium
4.8 g	Protein	5 mg	Cholesterol
24.9 g	Carbohydrates		

Spaghetti Salad I

—⁂—

1 package (10 ounces) spaghetti, cooked and drained
4 slices turkey bacon, cooked and crumbled
1 cup chopped broccoli, lightly steamed
¾ cup chopped carrots, lightly steamed
½ package (10 ounces) frozen green peas
1 small purple onion, chopped
3 stalks celery, chopped
1 teaspoon garlic salt
½ teaspoon seasoned salt
1 bottle (16 ounces) Kraft fat-free Honey Dijon
    salad dressing

In large bowl, combine all ingredients except salad dressing. After all ingredients are mixed and tossed, add half bottle dressing and toss. Chill. Just before serving, add remaining dressing and mix thoroughly.

Recipe makes 8 servings.

Each serving provides:

264	Calories	5.2 g	Dietary fiber
1.5 g	Fat	1016 mg	Sodium
9 g	Protein	5 mg	Cholesterol
52.5 g	Carbohydrates		

Mushroom and Beef Stew

⅓ pound fajita beef strips
1 small onion, chopped
1 can (14 ounces) beef broth, skim fat from top
¾ cup water
1 can (10¾ ounces) 98 percent fat-free cream of
    mushroom soup
2 cups fresh sliced mushrooms
2 tablespoons red cooking wine
1 tablespoon dry ranch dressing mix
1 tablespoon Lipton dry onion soup mix
Salt and black pepper to taste

Spray sauce pan with nonstick cooking spray. Brown
beef strips and onion. Add all remaining ingredients.
Simmer over very low heat for about 1 hour.

Recipe makes 6 servings.

Each serving provides:

103	Calories	0.8 g	Dietary fiber
3.7 g	Fat	778 mg	Sodium
7.7 g	Protein	18 mg	Cholesterol
8.6 g	Carbohydrates		

Cajun Bean Soup

———⚬———

3 cups dry mixed beans (pinto, navy, lima, black-eyed
    peas, lentils, split peas, kidney, garbanzo, etc.)
½ pound turkey sausage
1 cup onion, chopped
1 clove garlic, minced
1 can (16 ounces) tomatoes, undrained
1 tablespoon lemon juice
1–3 tablespoons Cajun seasoning

Wash beans; place in 3½-quart Crock Pot; cover
with water and soak overnight. Rinse and cover with
6–8 cups fresh water. Cook until beans are tender
(6–8 hours on low setting plus 2 hours on high setting).
    Brown turkey sausage in skillet, pouring off grease
as it accumulates. Place in colander; rinse with hot water
and add to beans.

Wipe out skillet and spray with nonstick cooking spray. Sauté onion and garlic until onion is clear; add to beans. Add tomatoes, lemon juice, and Cajun seasoning. Cook 30 minutes on high setting.

Note: Some of the bean juice may need to be removed from Crock Pot to make room for the tomatoes.

Recipe makes 14 servings. Serving size is 1 cup.

Each serving provides:

178	Calories	8 g	Dietary fiber
2.2 g	Fat	168 mg	Sodium
11.9 g	Protein	11 mg	Cholesterol
29 g	Carbohydrates		

Recipe Contributed by: Janet Potts, R.D., L.D.
Fitness/Wellness Dietitian
St. John Medical Center
Tulsa, Oklahoma

Pimiento Chicken Salad

Salad

2 cups cooked white chicken chunks
1 small onion, chopped
1 stalk celery, chopped
2 tablespoons chopped pimiento
1 apple, chopped
½ cup grated fat-free American cheese
Salt to taste

Dressing

½ cup fat-free Miracle Whip
⅓ cup (3 ounces) fat-free cream cheese

In large bowl, combine salad ingredients. In small bowl,
stir together dressing ingredients and mix until thoroughly blended. Pour dressing over salad and chill
1–2 hours before serving.

Recipe makes 6 servings.

Each serving provides:

149	Calories	1.3 g	Dietary fiber
1.6 g	Fat	448 mg	Sodium
18.8 g	Protein	40 mg	Cholesterol
14.3 g	Carbohydrates		

Buttermilk Coleslaw

Salad
6 cups shredded raw cabbage
½ medium green pepper, chopped fine
½ cup shredded carrot
⅛ teaspoon celery seed

Dressing
1 cup fat-free mayonnaise
¾ cup lowfat buttermilk
¼ cup sugar
Salt to taste

In large bowl, mix cabbage, green pepper, carrot, and celery seed.

In small bowl, gradually add buttermilk to mayonnaise. Mix in sugar gradually. Add salt. Stir dressing into salad mixture.

Recipe makes 10 servings.

Each serving provides:

58	Calories	1.2 g	Dietary fiber
0.3 g	Fat	334 mg	Sodium
1.2 g	Protein	1 mg	Cholesterol
13.7 g	Carbohydrates		

French Onion Soup

———✤———

3 medium onions, sliced
1 tablespoon flour
2 cans (14 ounces each) Swanson beef broth, defatted
1 cup water
2 teaspoons Molly McButter
¼ cup red cooking wine
½ teaspoon salt (optional)
Black pepper to taste
6 slices sourdough bread, toasted
6 slices Bordens' fat-free Swiss cheese

Preheat oven to 375 degrees F

In large skillet sprayed with nonstick cooking spray, brown onions until golden brown. Sprinkle flour over onions and continue browning and stirring.

In medium saucepan, combine beef broth, water, Molly McButter, wine, salt, and pepper. Add onions and simmer for 15–20 minutes.

Pour soup into individual bowls; top with 1 slice toast and 1 slice cheese. Warm at 375 degrees until cheese starts to melt. Serve immediately.

Recipe makes 6 servings.

Each serving provides:

170	Calories	2.8 g	Dietary fiber
0.5 g	Fat	861 mg	Sodium
11 g	Protein	2 mg	Cholesterol
28.3 g	Carbohydrates		

Italian Pasta Soup

———— ✦ ————

1 pound ground turkey breast or chicken breast
1 can (16 ounces) stewed tomatoes
1 can (15 ounces) kidney beans, drained and rinsed
½ cup canned or fresh julienne carrots
1 can (14 ounces) Swanson beef broth, defatted
1 can (8 ounces) tomato sauce
1 stalk celery, chopped
2 teaspoons dry onion flakes
1 clove garlic, pressed
1 cup uncooked pasta shells
1 package (1⅓ ounces) dry spaghetti sauce mix
1 package (2 ounces) dry ranch dressing mix
Salt and black pepper to taste
Dash of seasoned salt
3 cups water

Brown meat in large pot sprayed with nonstick cooking spray. Add remaining ingredients and simmer only long enough to cook pasta. Do not overcook. Serve warm with garlic toast.

Recipe makes 6 servings.

Each serving provides:

279	Calories	4.7 g	Dietary fiber
2 g	Fat	3472 mg	Sodium
28.6 g	Protein	46 mg	Cholesterol
37.3 g	Carbohydrates		

Sweet and Sour Chicken Salad

1 pound boneless, skinless chicken breasts,
    cut into small pieces
½ teaspoon garlic salt
Pineapple juice (reserved from tidbits below)
2 teaspoons lite soy sauce
½ large green pepper, chopped
1 medium white onion, chopped
¼ cup grated carrot
1 can (15¼ ounces) pineapple tidbits (save juice)
½ cup La Choy sweet and sour sauce

Brown chicken pieces in skillet sprayed with nonstick
cooking spray. Add garlic salt and continue cooking until
chicken is golden brown. Add juice from pineapple and
soy sauce; simmer and stir over medium-low heat until
all juice is absorbed. Set aside to cool.

In large bowl, combine vegetables and pineapple and toss. Add cooled chicken and mix. Pour on sweet and sour sauce and toss. Serve on a large lettuce leaf.

Recipe makes 6 servings.

Each serving provides:

193	Calories	1.5 g	Dietary fiber
1.4 g	Fat	361 mg	Sodium
19.2 g	Protein	46 mg	Cholesterol
25.9 g	Carbohydrates		

Taco Chicken Salad

—⁂—

1 pound boneless, skinless chicken breasts,
    cut into small pieces
1 package (1¼ ounces) taco seasoning
½ cup taco sauce
2 teaspoons dry onion flakes
1 cup canned whole-kernel corn, drained
¼ cup green chilies, chopped
½ cup fat-free sour cream
1 teaspoon dry ranch dressing mix

Add chicken pieces to skillet sprayed with nonstick
cooking spray. Sprinkle with taco seasoning and stir over
medium heat. Add taco sauce and onion flakes and stir.
Reduce heat to low and simmer until all liquid is cooked
into meat. Remove from heat and chill slightly.

Combine seasoned chicken with all remaining ingredients in medium-size bowl. Stir until thoroughly mixed and chill for a few hours before serving.

Serve on a bun or bagel as a sandwich. Can be rolled in flour or corn tortilla or served on a lettuce leaf and garnished with chopped tomatoes and grated fat-free cheese.

Recipe makes 6 servings.

Each serving provides:

140	Calories	0.9 g	Dietary fiber
1.3 g	Fat	492 mg	Sodium
21.2 g	Protein	46 mg	Cholesterol
10.9 g	Carbohydrates		

Summer Pasta Salad

Salad
1 package (12 ounces) tri-color rotelle pasta
8 ounces boneless, skinless chicken breasts,
    cut into small pieces
½ teaspoon garlic salt
Blackened or Cajun spices to taste

Dressing
3 cups (24 ounces) Kraft fat-free cream cheese
2 cloves garlic, pressed
½ cup cucumber, chopped
¾ teaspoon seasoned salt
2 teaspoons dry onion flakes

½ package (5 ounces) frozen Mandarin stir-fry
    vegetables, thawed

Cook pasta according to package directions. Drain,
rinse, and set aside to cool.
    Add chicken pieces to skillet sprayed with nonstick
cooking spray. Season with garlic salt and blackened
spices. Brown over medium heat until chicken is done.
Set aside to cool.

In food processor, combine all ingredients for dressing.

Pour half the dressing over pasta. Add thawed vegetables and chicken and toss. Refrigerate several hours. Add remaining dressing just before serving.

Recipe makes 6 large servings.

Each serving provides:

358	Calories	2.2 g	Dietary fiber
1.5 g	Fat	964 mg	Sodium
32.8 g	Protein	40 mg	Cholesterol
51.3 g	Carbohydrates		

Fruit Salad Deluxe

1 can (5¼ ounces) pineapple chunks, drained
1 can (16 ounces) dark sweet pitted cherries, drained
1 can (11 ounces) mandarin oranges, drained
1 cup green seedless grapes
1 cup fat-free sour cream
½ cup sugar
½ teaspoon vanilla extract
1 package (3 ounces) dry banana instant pudding mix
2 cups miniature marshmallows

In large bowl, combine all fruit. In another bowl, blend sour cream, sugar, and vanilla with electric mixer until sugar is dissolved. Pour over fruit and stir.

Stir in instant pudding mix and blend. Fold in marshmallows; chill and serve.

Recipe makes 8 servings.

Each serving provides:

194	Calories	1 g	Dietary fiber
0.2 g	Fat	221 mg	Sodium
2.8 g	Protein	0 mg	Cholesterol
47.3 g	Carbohydrates		

Creamy Southwest Soup

---

2 slices turkey bacon, cut into small pieces
1 medium onion, chopped
1 can (14 ounces) fat-free chicken broth
2 cans (16 ounces each) golden hominy, drained
2 cups water
1 can (4 ounces) chopped green chilies
1 clove garlic, pressed
Black pepper to taste
½ cup fat-free sour cream

Brown bacon and onion in large saucepan sprayed with nonstick cooking spray. Add all remaining ingredients except sour cream and simmer over medium heat about 20 minutes. Stir in sour cream just before serving.

Recipe makes 6 servings.

Each serving provides:

114	Calories	1.8 g	Dietary fiber
0.6 g	Fat	686 mg	Sodium
4.8 g	Protein	3 mg	Cholesterol
22.1 g	Carbohydrates		

Creamy Potatoes

—❧—

¾ cup (6 ounces) Kraft fat-free cream cheese
⅓ cup fat-free sour cream
¼ cup evaporated skim milk
⅓ cup plus 2 tablespoons fat-free Parmesan cheese
3 large potatoes, sliced
1 small onion, chopped
Garlic salt
Black pepper to taste
Molly McButter

Preheat oven to 350 degrees F

In medium bowl, combine cream cheese, sour cream, evaporated milk, and ⅓ cup Parmesan. Mix with electric mixer or food processor.

Line bottom of square casserole sprayed with nonstick cooking spray with layer of sliced potatoes and chopped onion. Sprinkle with garlic salt, pepper, and Molly McButter and drizzle a little cream sauce over top.

Repeat with several more layers until dish is almost full, saving enough sauce to cover top. Sprinkle top with 2 tablespoons Parmesan and Molly McButter. Cover and bake for 1 hour.

Recipe makes 6 servings.

Each serving provides:

210	Calories	3.4 g	Dietary fiber
0.2 g	Fat	245 mg	Sodium
10 g	Protein	9 mg	Cholesterol
41.3 g	Carbohydrates		

Chicken Salad Deluxe

½ cup (4 ounces) Kraft fat-free cream cheese
½ cup fat-free sour cream
½ teaspoon seasoned salt (optional)
½ teaspoon garlic salt or powder
Black pepper to taste
4 boneless, skinless chicken breasts, cooked and
    cut into small pieces
1 can (14 ounces) artichoke hearts, drained and
    quartered
1 jar (4 ounces) chopped pimientos
1 medium onion, chopped
½ cup chopped celery

In small bowl, combine cream cheese, sour cream, seasoned salt, garlic salt, and black pepper and stir. In large bowl, combine remaining ingredients.

Pour cream cheese mixture over chicken and vegetable mixture and toss. Chill and serve.

Recipe makes 6 servings.

Each serving provides:

159	Calories	1.6 g	Dietary fiber
2.3 g	Fat	435 mg	Sodium
23.5 g	Protein	52 mg	Cholesterol
10.3 g	Carbohydrates		

No-Oil Tabouli

———— ❧ ————

1 package (8 ounces) dry tabouli mix
1 cup cold water
1 cucumber, finely chopped
2 tomatoes, finely chopped
1 cup lemon juice
1 tablespoon dry onion flakes
1 teaspoon salt
1 teaspoon black pepper
½ cup Good Seasons fat-free Italian dressing (mixed
    according to package directions, using red wine
    vinegar)

In large bowl, combine tabouli mix and cold water. Stir
and let stand while combining remaining ingredients.
    Mix together remaining ingredients and add to
tabouli. Let stand in refrigerator at least 4 hours
before serving.

Recipe makes 10 servings.

Each serving provides:

95	Calories	3.1 g	Dietary fiber
0.1 g	Fat	505 mg	Sodium
3 g	Protein	0 mg	Cholesterol
22.1 g	Carbohydrates		

Spinach Cheese Bake

½ cup frozen chopped spinach, thawed and drained
1¾ cups fat-free cottage cheese
½ cup fat-free sour cream
⅓ cup fat-free liquid egg product
2 teaspoons dry onion flakes
2 tablespoons flour
Salt and black pepper to taste
¼ cup plus 2 tablespoons fat-free Parmesan cheese

Preheat oven to 325 degrees F

In large bowl, combine all ingredients except 2 tablespoons Parmesan and stir with spoon. Pour into 8- or 9-inch square baking dish sprayed with nonstick cooking spray and sprinkle reserved Parmesan over top. Bake for 30–40 minutes.

Recipe makes 6 servings.

Each serving provides:

99	Calories	0.6 g	Dietary fiber
0.1 g	Fat	328 mg	Sodium
13.1 g	Protein	9 mg	Cholesterol
10.8 g	Carbohydrates		

Peaches and Cream Gelatin Salad

1 can (29 ounces) sliced peaches, drained (save juice)
½ cup (4 ounces) fat-free cream cheese
⅓ cup fat-free sour cream
¼ cup sugar
1 package (3 ounces) peach-flavored gelatin

In food processor, combine ½ can drained peaches, cream cheese, sour cream, and sugar. Blend until smooth.

Add water to juice from peaches to make 1 cup and heat over medium heat until almost boiling. Remove from heat and add gelatin. Stir until dissolved. Cool slightly and combine with cream cheese mixture.

Add remaining peaches and pour into mold or dish and chill until set.

Recipe makes 6 servings.

Each serving provides:

169	Calories	1.7 g	Dietary fiber
0.1 g	Fat	141 mg	Sodium
5.5 g	Protein	3 mg	Cholesterol
38.9 g	Carbohydrates		

Green Chile–Artichoke Bake

———✦———

2 cans (14 ounces each) artichoke hearts
1 cup fat-free liquid egg product
½ cup evaporated skim milk
2 teaspoons Molly McButter
2 tablespoons flour
⅓ cup fat-free sour cream
1 can (4 ounces) chopped green chilies
2 teaspoons dry onion flakes
⅓ cup grated fat-free American or Cheddar cheese
Salt and black pepper to taste

Preheat oven to 350 degrees F

Drain artichoke hearts and cut into quarters.

In large bowl, combine egg product, evaporated milk, and Molly McButter, using electric mixer. Continue mixing and gradually add flour, then sour cream. Using spoon, stir in artichoke pieces, green chilies, onion flakes, and cheese. Add salt and black pepper.

Pour mixture into 9-inch casserole sprayed with nonstick cooking spray and bake for 45 minutes.

Recipe makes 6 servings.

Each serving provides:

101	Calories	1.4 g	Dietary fiber
0.4 g	Fat	463 mg	Sodium
10.9 g	Protein	2 mg	Cholesterol
14.5 g	Carbohydrates		

Broccoli and Cheese Soup

———— ❦ ————

1 can (14 ounces) fat-free chicken broth
1 package (10 ounces) frozen chopped broccoli
1 stalk celery, chopped
1 teaspoon dry onion flakes
½ cup evaporated skim milk
1 tablespoon Molly McButter
¼ cup fat-free sour cream
4 slices Kraft fat-free American cheese
Black pepper to taste

In medium saucepan, simmer chicken broth, broccoli,
celery, and onion flakes for 10 minutes. Add evaporated
milk, Molly McButter, and sour cream. Simmer
1 minute. Do not boil.

Break cheese into small pieces and drop into
soup. Stir and simmer until cheese melts. Add black
pepper. Serve.

Recipe makes 4 servings.

Each serving provides:

101	Calories	2.2 g	Dietary fiber
0.2 g	Fat	970 mg	Sodium
11.8 g	Protein	1 mg	Cholesterol
14.8 g	Carbohydrates		

Salmon Pasta Salad

—❦—

4 cups cooked pasta
1 can (6⅛ ounces) salmon, drained
½ medium onion, chopped
¾ cup chopped celery
½ red bell pepper, chopped
1 cup carrots, chopped and lightly steamed
1 teaspoon dill weed
1 tablespoon lemon juice
1½ cups fat-free ranch dressing

In large bowl, combine all ingredients except dressing and toss. Add half the dressing and toss. Chill and add remaining dressing just before serving.

Recipe makes 8 servings.

Each serving provides:

195	Calories	2 g	Dietary fiber
1.7 g	Fat	577 mg	Sodium
8.4 g	Protein	8 mg	Cholesterol
33.2 g	Carbohydrates		

Corn Chip Potato Salad

Dressing
½ cup fat-free mayonnaise
½ cup (4 ounces) Kraft fat-free cream cheese
½ teaspoon spicy mustard
½ teaspoon horseradish
1 clove garlic, pressed
¼ teaspoon black pepper

Salad
4 medium red potatoes, cooked and cubed
1 medium onion, chopped
⅓ cup chopped green pepper
⅓ cup chopped carrot
⅓ cup chopped celery
¾ cup crushed oil-free tortilla chips

In medium bowl, mix together all dressing ingredients.

In large bowl, combine potatoes, onion, green pepper, carrot, and celery. Pour dressing over vegetables and toss. Refrigerate 2–3 hours before serving. Just before serving, sprinkle tortilla chips over each serving.

Recipe makes 6 servings.

Each serving provides:

151	Calories	3.2 g	Dietary fiber
0.4 g	Fat	361 mg	Sodium
5.2 g	Protein	3 mg	Cholesterol
32.2 g	Carbohydrates		

Creamy Oven Hash Browns

―❦―

1 can (10¾ ounces) Campbell's 98 percent fat-free
    cream of mushroom soup
1¼ cups fat-free chicken broth
½ cup fat-free sour cream
1 tablespoon Molly McButter
Salt and black pepper to taste
1 package (24 ounces) O'Brien frozen hash brown
    potatoes (with green peppers and onions)
½ cup fat-free Parmesan cheese

Preheat oven to 350 degrees F

In large bowl, combine soup, chicken broth, sour cream,
Molly McButter, salt, and pepper; mix thoroughly. Add
hash brown potatoes and mix.

Pour into 9- × 13-inch baking dish sprayed with
nonstick cooking spray. Sprinkle Parmesan on top and
bake for 40–45 minutes.

Recipe makes 9 servings.

Each serving provides:

106	Calories	1.4 g	Dietary fiber
0.7 g	Fat	430 mg	Sodium
3.8 g	Protein	4 mg	Cholesterol
20.4 g	Carbohydrates		

Fancy Mashed Potatoes

———✥———

Mashed potato flakes
1 tablespoon Molly McButter
Evaporated skim milk
2 slices turkey bacon, cooked and crumbled
⅓ cup fat-free sour cream
1 tablespoon dry ranch dressing mix
1 green onion, sliced thin

Prepare mashed potatoes according to package
directions for 4 servings. Omit butter or margarine
and use Molly McButter. Use evaporated skim milk.
Add bacon, sour cream, ranch dressing mix, and onion.
Mix thoroughly. Serve warm.

Recipe makes 4 servings.

Each serving provides:

111	Calories	0.3 g	Dietary fiber
0.8 g	Fat	535 mg	Sodium
6.7 g	Protein	6 mg	Cholesterol
19.3 g	Carbohydrates		

Old-Fashioned Baked Beans

2 cans (15 ounces each) pinto or navy beans,
    partially drained
½ cup dark brown sugar
⅓ cup ketchup
¼ teaspoon liquid smoke
2 teaspoons dry onion flakes
2 slices turkey bacon, cut in half

Preheat oven to 350 degrees F

In large bowl, combine all ingredients except bacon and
mix thoroughly. Pour into baking dish sprayed with
nonstick cooking spray and lay bacon slices on top.
Bake for 45–55 minutes.

Recipe makes 6 servings.

Each serving provides:

187	Calories	5.7 g	Dietary fiber
0.9 g	Fat	399 mg	Sodium
6.5 g	Protein	3 mg	Cholesterol
40.3 g	Carbohydrates		

Sweet Potato French Fries

3 medium, fresh sweet potatoes
Nonfat butter-flavored nonstick cooking spray
¼ cup sugar
½ teaspoon cinnamon*

Preheat oven to 375 degrees F

Peel and slice sweet potatoes like French fries. Spread
on baking sheet sprayed with nonstick cooking spray
and lightly spray potatoes.

In small bowl, mix together sugar and cinnamon.
Sprinkle over potatoes and bake for 20–25 minutes
or until tender.

Recipe makes 3 servings.

Each serving provides:

181	Calories	3.6 g	Dietary fiber
0.3 g	Fat	12 mg	Sodium
2 g	Protein	0 mg	Cholesterol
43.8 g	Carbohydrates		

---

*You may use seasoned salt as an alternate seasoning for sugar and
cinnamon.

Black-Eyed Pea and Corn Salad

Salad
1 can (16 ounces) black-eyed peas, drained
1 can (16 ounces) whole-kernel corn, drained
1 can (14 ounces) artichoke hearts in water, drained
    and quartered
1 small onion, chopped
½ cup chopped celery
½ small green pepper, chopped
Black pepper to taste

Dressing
1 cup (8 ounces) Kraft fat-free cream cheese
½ teaspoon horseradish
1 clove garlic, pressed
½ teaspoon seasoned salt (optional)

In large bowl, combine all salad ingredients. In small bowl, combine all dressing ingredients and mix thoroughly. Pour dressing over salad and chill several hours before serving.

Recipe makes 6 servings.

Each serving provides:

133	Calories	3.5 g	Dietary fiber
1 g	Fat	502 mg	Sodium
8.9 g	Protein	5 mg	Cholesterol
24.5 g	Carbohydrates		

Bean Salad

Salad
1 can (15 ounces) white beans, drained and rinsed
1 can (15 ounces) red kidney beans, drained and rinsed
1 small onion, chopped
½ cup chopped celery
½ bell pepper, chopped
½ medium cucumber, chopped
4 radishes, sliced

Dressing
1 cup (8 ounces) Kraft fat-free cream cheese
1 tablespoon tomato paste
¼ teaspoon lite soy sauce
1 clove garlic, pressed
¼ teaspoon seasoned salt (optional)

In large bowl, combine all salad ingredients. In small bowl, combine all dressing ingredients and pour over salad. Chill before serving.

Recipe makes 6 servings.

Each serving provides:

182	Calories	6.4 g	Dietary fiber
0.5 g	Fat	667 mg	Sodium
14.2 g	Protein	6 mg	Cholesterol
31.1 g	Carbohydrates		

Stuffed Tomatoes

—❦—

4 large tomatoes
1¼ cups cooked rice
4 slices turkey bacon, cooked and crumbled
2 green onions, chopped
½ cup shredded fat-free American or Cheddar cheese
2 teaspoons Molly McButter
5 drops Tabasco sauce
⅛ teaspoon garlic powder
Salt and black pepper to taste

Preheat oven to 350 degrees F

Slice top off each tomato and remove pulp. Combine
remaining ingredients and mix well. Stuff tomatoes with
rice mixture and bake for 25 minutes in baking dish
sprayed with nonstick cooking spray.

These may also be served unbaked and chilled;
however, I prefer them baked.

Recipe makes 4 servings.

Each serving provides:

162	Calories	2.1 g	Dietary fiber
2.1 g	Fat	396 mg	Sodium
10 g	Protein	13 mg	Cholesterol
26.4 g	Carbohydrates		

Julie's Potatoes

—✦—

¾ cups fat-free sour cream
1 small onion, chopped
2 teaspoons Molly McButter
⅓ cup light Cheez Whiz
4 large potatoes, thinly sliced
Salt and black pepper to taste
1 cups crushed cornflakes

Preheat oven to 425 degrees F

In medium bowl, combine sour cream, onion, Molly McButter, and Cheez Whiz and stir with spoon. In large bowl, pour sour cream mixture over potatoes and stir. Pour into a square casserole sprayed with nonstick cooking spray. Add salt and pepper and bake for 1 hour. Top with cornflakes for the last 10 minutes of cooking.

Recipe makes 8 servings.

Each serving provides:

210	Calories	3.5 g	Dietary fiber
1.2 g	Fat	330 mg	Sodium
7.1 g	Protein	5 mg	Cholesterol
43.3 g	Carbohydrates		

Recipe Contributed by: Julie Finley

Cajun Seafood Salad

—◆—

½ cup fat-free Italian dressing
1 tablespoon spicy hot mustard
1 cup cooked shrimp or lobster pieces
2 cups cooked rice
6 green onions, chopped
2 stalks celery, chopped
2 tablespoons dill pickle relish
2 tablespoons sweet pickle relish
1 teaspoon Louisiana hot sauce
½ teaspoon seasoned salt
¼ teaspoon garlic salt

In small bowl, combine Italian dressing and mustard and stir until blended. In large bowl, combine remaining ingredients. Add dressing; chill and serve.

Recipe makes 6 servings.

Each serving provides:

136	Calories	1.1 g	Dietary fiber
0.7 g	Fat	451 mg	Sodium
7.5 g	Protein	46 mg	Cholesterol
24.8 g	Carbohydrates		

Layered Pea Salad

—✦—

1½ cups fat-free cottage cheese
3 cups shredded lettuce
1 can (16 ounces) black-eyed peas
1 cup shredded fat-free cheese
1 small red onion, thinly sliced
1 package(10 ounces) frozen green peas
½ bell pepper, sliced
1 cup fat-free Italian dressing

If possible, use a clear glass 2-quart straight-sided bowl in which to layer salad.

Start with a layer of half the cottage cheese, then add half the lettuce, all the black-eyed peas, all the cheese and onion, the remaining lettuce, all the green peas, the remaining cottage cheese, and all the bell pepper. Pour dressing over top; chill and serve.

Recipe makes 8 servings.

Each serving provides:

138	Calories	4.2 g	Dietary fiber
0.4 g	Fat	472 mg	Sodium
14.9 g	Protein	6 mg	Cholesterol
19.3 g	Carbohydrates		

Eggplant Parmesan

---

1 medium eggplant, peeled and sliced into
    ½-inch-thick slices
2 egg whites, slightly beaten
2 cups crushed cornflakes
¾ cup fat-free Parmesan cheese
½ cup shredded fat-free mozzarella cheese
1 can stewed chopped tomatoes
1 small onion, chopped
1 teaspoon garlic powder
Black pepper to taste

Preheat oven to 350 degrees F

Dip eggplant slices in egg white and roll in cornflakes.
Brown lightly in skillet sprayed with nonstick cooking
spray.

Place browned eggplant in large casserole sprayed with nonstick cooking spray. Sprinkle with Parmesan and mozzarella cheese. Gently pour tomatoes over entire casserole. Sprinkle onions over top and season with garlic powder and black pepper. Bake for 45–50 minutes.

Recipe makes 6 servings.

Each serving provides:

189	Calories	4 g	Dietary fiber
0.4 g	Fat	650 mg	Sodium
9.7 g	Protein	8 mg	Cholesterol
36.8 g	Carbohydrates		

Seafood Rice Salad

---❦---

Dressing
²⁄₃ cup (6½ ounces) Kraft fat-free cream cheese
¼ cup fat-free mayonnaise
1 clove garlic, pressed
1 tablespoon lemon juice
¼ teaspoon seasoned salt

Salad
4 cups cooked rice
1 cup imitation lobster meat, cut into small pieces
1 can (14 ounces) artichoke hearts in water, drained
      and quartered
1 can (16 ounces) whole kernel corn, drained
3 green onions, chopped
½ small green pepper, chopped
2 tablespoons chopped pimientos
½ teaspoon dill weed
Black pepper to taste

Combine all dressing ingredients in food processor or blender. Blend until smooth and set aside.

In large bowl, combine all salad ingredients and toss. Add dressing and toss. Chill 1 hour before serving.

Recipe makes 6 servings.

Each serving provides:

295	Calories	2.5 g	Dietary fiber
1.4 g	Fat	685 mg	Sodium
12.2 g	Protein	6 mg	Cholesterol
58.8 g	Carbohydrates		

Festive Taco Corn

———— ✥ ————

1 package (16 ounces) frozen corn
2 fresh green chilies, chopped
1 tablespoon Molly McButter
1 teaspoon dry taco seasoning
2 teaspoons dry onion flakes
½ cup water

In medium saucepan, combine all ingredients. Simmer over low heat until corn is done and most of the water has cooked away.

Recipe makes 8 servings.

Each serving provides:

55	Calories	1.7 g	Dietary fiber
0.3 g	Fat	98 mg	Sodium
1.9 g	Protein	0 mg	Cholesterol
13.2 g	Carbohydrates		

Wilted Lettuce Salad

⅓ cup evaporated skim milk
1 teaspoon dry mustard
¼ teaspoon black pepper
5–6 cups leaf lettuce
1 green onion, chopped
4 slices turkey bacon
6 tablespoons vinegar
2 teaspoons sugar

Mix together evaporated milk, mustard, and black pepper. Combine lettuce and onion and pour skim milk mixture over top. Toss and chill 30–60 minutes.

In skillet sprayed with nonstick cooking spray, brown bacon. Cool and crumble. Add vinegar and sugar to skillet and bring almost to boil. Pour over lettuce. Top with crumbled bacon and serve warm.

Recipe makes 4 servings.

Each serving provides:

67	Calories	1.4 g	Dietary fiber
1.9 g	Fat	222 mg	Sodium
5.1 g	Protein	11 mg	Cholesterol
8.8 g	Carbohydrates		

Spaghetti Salad II

Salad
1 package (12 ounces) spaghetti
1 cup fresh broccoli, chopped
1 cup frozen peas
1 medium onion, chopped
1 green pepper, chopped
1 fresh tomato, chopped
1 carrot, grated
1 tablespoon chopped pimientos
½ cup grated fat-free cheese

Dressing
1 package (4.3 ounces) dry Lipton onion soup mix
½ cup 99 percent fat-free tomato soup
1 cup fat-free Italian dressing

Break spaghetti into 3- to 4-inch pieces; cook according to package directions, drain, and rinse. In large bowl, combine all salad ingredients and toss.

Combine all dressing ingredients and pour a portion over spaghetti mixture and chill. Add additional dressing just before serving.

Recipe makes 8 servings.

Each serving provides:

254	Calories	4.6 g	Dietary fiber
1.6 g	Fat	649 mg	Sodium
10.7 g	Protein	2 mg	Cholesterol
49.7 g	Carbohydrates		

Oven-Fried Okra

—◆—

Nonfat butter-flavored nonstick cooking spray
1 package (24 ounces) frozen breaded okra*
Salt and black pepper to taste

Preheat oven to 375 degrees F

Spray baking sheet with cooking spray and spread okra over entire sheet; spray lightly and season with salt and pepper. Bake for 45–50 minutes or until golden brown.

Recipe makes 6 servings.

Each serving provides:

95	Calories	1.3 g	Dietary fiber
1.5 g	Fat	333 mg	Sodium
2.7 g	Protein	0 mg	Cholesterol
18.6 g	Carbohydrates		

---

*Use only frozen breaded okra that has not been prefried.

Main Dishes and Casseroles

Chicken Breast Marinade

Biscuits and Sausage Gravy

Creamed Corn Casserole

"Birdie's" Barley

Chili

Mexican Lasagna

Eggplant Casserole

Mushroom Meat Loaf

Seafood Fettuccini

Vegetarian Lasagna

Stuffed Potato Skins

Hominy and Black-Eyed Pea Casserole

Hominy Casserole

Stuffed Peppers

Chicken with Honey Mustard Sauce

Hungarian Chicken Goulash

Sausage and Rice Casserole

Orange Sweet Potato Casserole

Onion Smothered Chicken

Erma's Chicken with Curry Sauce

Ranch Dinner

Lite Reuben Sandwich

Beef and Noodle Casserole

Chicken Breasts with Wine Sauce

Chicken-Fried Chicken with Cream Gravy

Oven-Fried Chicken Breasts

Broccoli and Rice Casserole

Orange Shrimp

Green Chile Rice

Taco Tamale Pie

Chicken Breasts with Apricot–Orange Sauce

Tabasco Chicken

French Onion Chicken and Potato Bake

Barbecue Chicken and Coleslaw Sandwich

Pimiento Chicken

Honey Dijon Oven Chicken

Savory Apricot Chicken

Jalapeño Chicken

Clam Linguine

Noodle Casserole

Rotel Chicken with Sour Cream

Onion-Mushroom Meat Loaf

Lemon Garlic Pasta

Focaccia with Roasted Garlic and Onion

Quick and Easy Chicken Kebabs

Onion Cheese Pie

Parmesan Noodles

Oven Crispy Onion–Mushroom Chicken

Honey Crunchy Chicken

Crispy Honey Dijon Chicken

Creole Gravy Chicken with Rice

Chili Dogs in a Blanket

Corn Quiche

Breakfast Burrito

Chicken Gumbo

Spinach and Carrot Quiche

Stuffed Bell Peppers

Mexican Burgers

Philly Turkey with Swiss on a Bagel

Tuna Lasagna

Old-Fashioned Homestyle Noodles

Tortilla Casserole

Cauliflower and Broccoli Stir-Fry

Crispy Buttermilk Chicken

Vegetable Fajitas

Salmon Cakes

Cream Cheese Chicken Salad Pockets

White Chili

Pasta–Vegetable Casserole

Chilled Cream Cheese Veggie Pizza

Blackened Orange Shrimp

Chicken Marsala with Angel Hair Pasta

Pizza Burger

Spicy Oven Chicken

Spaghetti Casserole

Egg Foo Yung

Chicken Gumbo Burgers

Sweet Onion Sandwich

Pasta Salad with Honey Mustard Chicken

Ham, Cheese, and Asparagus Rolls

Bacon with Brown Sugar

Shrimp Fettuccini with Creamy Cheese Sauce

Tostadas

Shrimp Rockefeller

Oven Lemon-Pepper Chicken

Blackened Chicken Pasta

Rockefeller Casserole

Chicken with Lemon Cream Sauce

Pasta Primavera

Breakfast Pizzas

Creamy Chicken and Artichoke Hearts over Noodles

Santa Fe Pizza

Hot Brown Sandwich

Vegetarian Enchiladas

Orange Marmalade Chicken

Chicken Breast Marinade

½ teaspoon sesame seeds
¼ cup orange juice concentrate
1 tablespoon lemon juice
4 tablespoons lite soy sauce
3 green onions, chopped
2 teaspoons grated fresh ginger root
1 teaspoon red pepper flakes
4 boneless, skinless chicken breasts

Brown sesame seeds over medium-low heat in small pan sprayed with nonstick cooking spray. In shallow bowl, mix together remaining ingredients except chicken. Add sesame seeds.

Marinate chicken breasts in mixture 30–60 minutes in refrigerator, turning occasionally. Cook in oven or on outdoor grill. Discard remaining marinade.

Recipe makes 4 servings.

Each serving provides:

174	Calories	0.6 g	Dietary fiber
1.7 g	Fat	684 mg	Sodium
28.9 g	Protein	68 mg	Cholesterol
8.9 g	Carbohydrates		

Biscuits and Sausage Gravy

Biscuits
Use refrigerated canned biscuits that are either fat free
or 1 gram fat per biscuit; or make your own with
Pioneer Low-Fat Biscuit Mix or a lite biscuit mix.
My favorite, of course, is the Pioneer Low-Fat
Biscuit Mix because of the excellent quality and
taste. Prepare according to package directions.

Gravy
1 ounce ground turkey sausage
4 tablespoons flour
1 cup fat free chicken broth
½ cup evaporated skim milk
1 cup skim milk
2 teaspoons Molly McButter
Salt and black pepper to taste

In large skillet sprayed with nonstick cooking spray, brown turkey sausage. Add flour and lightly brown. In medium bowl, combine remaining ingredients. Stir with whisk and add to sausage mixture; stir until gravy thickens. Serve over hot biscuits.

Recipe makes 6 servings. (Nutritional information based on gravy only.)

Each serving provides:

119	Calories	0.1 g	Dietary fiber
1.5 g	Fat	588 mg	Sodium
6.1 g	Protein	5 mg	Cholesterol
20 g	Carbohydrates		

Creamed Corn Casserole

1 can (16 ounces) cream-style corn
½ cup fat-free liquid egg product
2 teaspoons dry onion flakes
2 tablespoons finely chopped green pepper
1 teaspoon Molly McButter
Salt and black pepper to taste
1 cup cornflakes, crushed

Preheat oven to 350 degrees F

Combine corn, egg product, onion flakes, green pepper, Molly McButter, salt, and pepper. Pour into baking dish sprayed with nonstick cooking spray and top with crushed cornflakes. Bake for 50–55 minutes.

Recipe makes 4 servings.

Each serving provides:

141	Calories	2 g	Dietary fiber
0.7 g	Fat	543 mg	Sodium
5.9 g	Protein	0 mg	Cholesterol
31.5 g	Carbohydrates		

"Birdie's" Barley

1 cup barley
1 medium onion, chopped
2 stalks celery, chopped
1 can (10½ ounces) consommé
1 soup can water
Salt and black pepper to taste

Preheat oven to 350 degrees F

Brown barley in skillet sprayed with nonstick cooking
spray and pour into a casserole dish. Brown onion and
celery and add to barley. Add consommé, water, salt, and
pepper. Cover and bake for approximately 1 hour or
until all liquid has been absorbed.

Recipe makes 6 servings.

Each serving provides:

137	Calories	6.2 g	Dietary fiber
0.8 g	Fat	280 mg	Sodium
6.6 g	Protein	0 mg	Cholesterol
26.8 g	Carbohydrates		

Chili

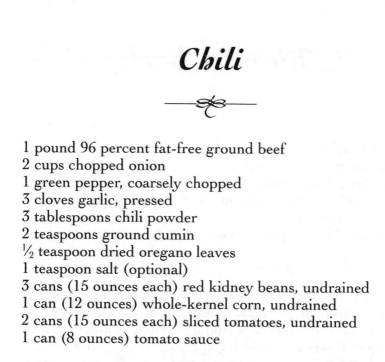

1 pound 96 percent fat-free ground beef
2 cups chopped onion
1 green pepper, coarsely chopped
3 cloves garlic, pressed
3 tablespoons chili powder
2 teaspoons ground cumin
½ teaspoon dried oregano leaves
1 teaspoon salt (optional)
3 cans (15 ounces each) red kidney beans, undrained
1 can (12 ounces) whole-kernel corn, undrained
2 cans (15 ounces each) sliced tomatoes, undrained
1 can (8 ounces) tomato sauce

Brown ground beef in Dutch oven; drain. Add onion, green pepper, garlic, chili powder, cumin, oregano, and salt; mix well. Cook, stirring, until onion and pepper are tender.

Add beans, corn, tomatoes, and tomato sauce; stir to mix well, breaking up tomatoes with a fork. Cover and simmer gently, stirring occasionally, until thickened and flavors are well blended (about 30 minutes).

Variation: May be served on baked potato or over pasta.

Recipe makes 13 servings. Serving size is 1 cup.

Each serving provides:

195	Calories	6.6 g	Dietary fiber
2.7 g	Fat	668 mg	Sodium
15.7 g	Protein	19 mg	Cholesterol
28.9 g	Carbohydrates		

Recipe Contributed by: Janet Potts, R.D., L.D.
Fitness/Wellness Dietitian
St. John Medical Center
Tulsa, Oklahoma

Mexican Lasagna

⅓ pound extra lean ground beef
⅓ cup water
1 bunch green onions, chopped
1 package (1¼ ounces) taco seasoning
1 cup 1 percent cottage cheese
¼ cup fat-free liquid egg product
3 tablespoons chopped green chilies
6 soft corn tortillas
1½ cups frozen corn, thawed
½ cup Sargento light grated Cheddar cheese

Preheat oven to 350 degrees F

Spray skillet with nonstick cooking spray. Add ground beef and brown over medium heat. Add water, green onions, and taco seasoning and stir. Set aside.

In medium bowl, combine cottage cheese, liquid egg product, and green chilies.

Spray 7 × 11 inch casserole dish with nonstick cooking spray. Spread corn tortillas over bottom and partially up the sides of the casserole dish. Spoon meat mixture in first. Add all of the corn for the next layer. Add cottage cheese mixture and top with grated Cheddar cheese. Bake for 35–40 minutes.

Recipe makes 4 servings.

Each serving provides:

332	Calories	5.5 g	Dietary fiber
8 g	Fat	1106 mg	Sodium
25.7 g	Protein	30 mg	Cholesterol
40.8 g	Carbohydrates		

Eggplant Casserole

1 medium-large eggplant, peeled and diced
1 teaspoon salt
1 box (6 ounces) Kellogg's stuffing mix croutons
1 medium onion, chopped
⅓ cup fat-free Parmesan cheese
2 teaspoons Molly McButter
¾ cup fat-free chicken broth
¾ cup fat-free liquid egg product
Salt and black pepper to taste

Preheat oven to 350 degrees F

Cover eggplant with water, add salt, and simmer over low heat until tender, 10–15 minutes. Drain and set aside to cool.

Combine eggplant with remaining ingredients and mix. Pour into square or round baking dish sprayed with nonstick cooking spray and bake for 45–50 minutes.

Recipe makes 6 servings.

Each serving provides:

163	Calories	2.6 g	Dietary fiber
0.3 g	Fat	1005 mg	Sodium
8.4 g	Protein	3 mg	Cholesterol
31.4 g	Carbohydrates		

Mushroom Meat Loaf

---

1 pound ground turkey breast
½ cup finely chopped fresh mushrooms
⅓ cup fat-free liquid egg product
1 can (10¾ ounces) 98 percent fat-free condensed
    Cream of Mushroom Soup
2 tablespoons fat-free sour cream
2 teaspoons dry onion flakes
Salt and black pepper to taste
½ cup Sargento light grated Cheddar cheese

Preheat oven to 375 degrees F

In large bowl, combine all ingredients except cheese
and mix thoroughly.
        Spray loaf pan with nonstick cooking spray.
Place meat loaf mixture in pan. Bake for 60–70 minutes.
Add grated cheese to top of loaf 10–15 minutes before
removing from oven.

Recipe makes 8 servings.

Each serving provides:

113	Calories	0.1 g	Dietary fiber
2.7 g	Fat	269 mg	Sodium
17.2 g	Protein	38 mg	Cholesterol
4.4 g	Carbohydrates		

Seafood Fettuccini

———⊰❦⊱———

2 tablespoons chopped fresh garlic
1/4 cup white cooking wine
1/2 cup fat-free plain yogurt
1/2 cup fat-free sour cream
1/4 cup skim milk
1/2 cup fat-free Parmesan cheese
1 teaspoon nutmeg
1 can (6 ounces) medium deveined shrimp
1 can (6 ounces) white crab meat
1 package (12 ounces) fettuccini pasta
Salt and black pepper to taste
Parsley and lemon for garnish

Sauté garlic in wine on low heat 1–2 minutes. Add yogurt, sour cream, skim milk, Parmesan, and nutmeg. Bring to boil; reduce heat and simmer. Add shrimp and crab meat; stir until well blended and let simmer 10–15 minutes.

Cook pasta according to package directions. Add to sauce and stir well. Season with salt and pepper. Serve immediately. Garnish with parsley and a slice of lemon.

Recipe makes 4 servings.

Each serving provides:

521	Calories	3.9 g	Dietary fiber
3.1 g	Fat	444 mg	Sodium
36.4 g	Protein	118 mg	Cholesterol
81.8 g	Carbohydrates		

Recipe Contributed by: Jana R. Love, M.S.
Manager, Therapeutic Exercise Services
St. John Medical Center
Tulsa, Oklahoma

Vegetarian Lasagna

—✥—

10 lasagna noodles, cooked and drained
1 large onion, chopped
1 bell pepper, sliced (red is pretty in this recipe)
2 cups (½ pound) fresh mushrooms, sliced
1 zucchini, sliced
1 cup sliced carrots
1 jar (26 ounces) Healthy Choice spaghetti sauce
1 can (14½ ounces) diced tomatoes
1 teaspoon dried basil
1 teaspoon garlic powder
1 teaspoon oregano
½ teaspoon marjoram
1 teaspoon seasoned salt
⅓ cup fat-free liquid egg product
1 carton (24 ounces) fat-free cottage cheese
1 cup grated fat-free mozzarella cheese
½ cup fat-free Parmesan cheese

Preheat oven to 350 degrees F

Prepare lasagna noodles according to package directions.

Brown all vegetables in large skillet sprayed with nonstick cooking spray and simmer until almost tender (about 10 minutes).

In large bowl, combine spaghetti sauce, tomatoes, and spices. In medium bowl, stir together egg product and cottage cheese.

In 9 × 13 inch glass baking dish sprayed with nonstick cooking spray, layer the noodles, half the cooked vegetables, half the cottage cheese mixture, half the tomato mixture, and half the mozzarella cheese.

Repeat layers, ending with remaining mozzarella cheese, and top with Parmesan. Cover and bake for 1 hour.

Recipe makes 8 servings.

Each serving provides:

272	Calories	4.9 g	Dietary fiber
0.9 g	Fat	960 mg	Sodium
21.5 g	Protein	11 mg	Cholesterol
44.6 g	Carbohydrates		

Stuffed Potato Skins

5 medium baking potatoes
1 pound boneless, skinless chicken breasts,
    cut into small pieces
1 cup (¼ pound) fresh mushrooms, sliced
1 small onion, chopped
½ green pepper, chopped
1 can (10¾ ounces) Campbell's 98 percent fat-free
    cream of mushroom soup
½ cup fat-free sour cream
¼ teaspoon garlic powder
Salt and black pepper to taste
Paprika

Preheat oven to 425 degrees F

Bake potatoes at 425 degrees about 1 hour or until
done. Cool on rack until cool enough to handle. Slice
each in half lengthwise and remove some potato from
center. Leave enough around edges so potato will keep
its shape.

Brown chicken pieces in skillet sprayed with nonstick cooking spray. Add mushrooms, onion, and green pepper and brown. Drain off any excess liquid. Add mushroom soup, sour cream, garlic powder, salt, and pepper. Stir until mixed thoroughly. Spoon into potato halves.

Place stuffed potatoes on baking sheet sprayed with nonstick cooking spray and sprinkle paprika on top. Bake at 350 degrees for 25–30 minutes.

Note: Save potato centers to mash or make potato cubes for another meal.

Recipe makes 5 servings.

Each serving provides:

386	Calories	5.7 g	Dietary fiber
2.5 g	Fat	350 mg	Sodium
28.5 g	Protein	55 mg	Cholesterol
62 g	Carbohydrates		

Hominy and Black-Eyed Pea Casserole

½ can Campbell's creamy onion soup
¼ cup fat-free chicken broth
⅓ cup fat-free sour cream
¼ teaspoon garlic powder
¼ teaspoon chili powder
2 cans (16 ounces each) golden hominy, drained
1 can (15 ounces) black-eyed peas, drained
Salt and black pepper to taste
½ cup grated fat-free cheese

Preheat oven to 350 degrees F

In large bowl, combine soup, chicken broth, sour cream, garlic powder, and chili powder; mix well. Add hominy and black-eyed peas and mix. Pour into casserole sprayed with nonstick cooking spray. Add salt and pepper and top with grated cheese. Bake for 30 minutes.

Recipe makes 8 servings.

Each serving provides:

116	Calories	2.4 g	Dietary fiber
1.1 g	Fat	576 mg	Sodium
6 g	Protein	4 mg	Cholesterol
20.4 g	Carbohydrates		

Hominy Casserole

2 cans (16 ounces) hominy
1 small onion, chopped
1 jar (4 ounces) chopped pimientos
1 can (10¾ ounces) Campbell's 98 percent fat-free
    cream of mushroom soup
1 can (4 ounces) sliced mushrooms, drained
½ cup fat-free chicken broth
½ cup fat-free sour cream
1 tablespoon Molly McButter
½ cup shredded fat-free mozzarella cheese
Salt and black pepper to taste
½ cup crushed cornflakes

Preheat oven to 350 degrees F

Combine all ingredients except cornflakes and mix
thoroughly. Pour into small casserole sprayed with
nonstick cooking spray. Top with crushed cornflakes
and bake for 35–45 minutes.

Recipe makes 8 servings.

Each serving provides:

142	Calories	2.1 g	Dietary fiber
0.8 g	Fat	764 mg	Sodium
6.2 g	Protein	3 mg	Cholesterol
27.3 g	Carbohydrates		

Stuffed Peppers

½ pound 96 percent fat-free ground beef
1 can (14½ ounces) Italian-style tomatoes
½ cup water
1 teaspoon Italian seasoning
½ teaspoon salt (optional)
1½ cups instant rice, uncooked
4 large bell peppers

Preheat oven to 350 degrees F

Brown ground beef in large skillet; drain grease, if any. Add tomatoes, water, Italian seasoning, and salt. Bring to boil. Stir in instant rice. Cover; remove from heat and let stand 5 minutes or until rice has absorbed liquid.

Cut each pepper in half lengthwise and remove stem and seeds. Place in baking dish and fill with rice mixture. Bake for 30 minutes or until peppers are tender-crisp.

Variation: Omit baking and store unbaked stuffed peppers in refrigerator until ready for use. Microwave individual peppers on high for 2 minutes.

Recipe makes 4 servings.

Each serving provides:

257	Calories	3.9 g	Dietary fiber
2.8 g	Fat	207 mg	Sodium
15.9 g	Protein	28 mg	Cholesterol
42.2 g	Carbohydrates		

Recipe Contributed by: Janet Potts, R.D., L.D.
Fitness/Wellness Dietitian
St. John Medical Center
Tulsa, Oklahoma

Chicken with Honey Mustard Sauce

4 boneless, skinless chicken breasts (3 ounces each)
½ teaspoon garlic powder
½ teaspoon onion powder
Salt and black pepper to taste
½ cup fat-free chicken broth
2 tablespoons honey
2 tablespoons Dijon mustard
½ teaspoon Molly McButter
Dash of lite soy sauce

Season both sides of chicken breasts with garlic powder, onion powder, salt, and pepper.

Spray skillet with nonstick cooking spray. Brown and cook chicken breasts over low-medium heat until done. Remove chicken from skillet.

Add chicken broth, honey, mustard, Molly McButter, and soy sauce. Stir over low heat. Pour sauce over chicken before serving.

Recipe makes 4 servings.

Each serving provides:

138	Calories	0.1 g	Dietary fiber
1.6 g	Fat	405 mg	Sodium
20.4 g	Protein	49 mg	Cholesterol
9.8 g	Carbohydrates		

Hungarian Chicken Goulash

—⚬—

3 large onions, coarsely chopped (about 3 cups)
2 tablespoons paprika
2 skinless chicken breasts (leave on bone)
1 teaspoon salt
2 potatoes, peeled and quartered
$1\frac{1}{2}$ cups water

In Dutch oven lightly sprayed with nonstick cooking spray, sauté onions until brown. Remove from heat; cool, add paprika, and mix well. Return to heat and add chicken, turning so all pieces are coated with onion mixture. Sprinkle with salt; cover and simmer 1 hour, stirring occasionally and adding water if necessary. Add potatoes and 1½ cups water. Cook 45 minutes, adding more water if necessary. Serve with dumplings or rice.

Recipe makes 4 servings.

Each serving provides:

232	Calories	5.2 g	Dietary fiber
1.5 g	Fat	580 mg	Sodium
17.9 g	Protein	34 mg	Cholesterol
37.6 g	Carbohydrates		

Original Recipe by: Rose Merle with modifications by
    Linda Merle, R.N. II
Healthy LifeStyle Programs System Manager
St. John Medical Center
Tulsa, Oklahoma

Sausage and Rice Casserole

———&———

1 roll (12 ounces) ground turkey sausage
1 green pepper, chopped
6 green onions, chopped
1 small bunch celery, chopped
Salt and black pepper to taste
2 packages (3 ounces each) dry chicken noodle soup
    (Ramen lowfat noodles)
$4\frac{1}{2}$ cups boiling water
1 cup brown rice, uncooked
1 can (8 ounces) water chestnuts, drained
1 cup fat-free sour cream

Preheat oven to 350 degrees F

Brown turkey sausage; drain, rinse with hot water, and return to skillet. Add green pepper, onions, and celery and sauté 5–10 minutes. Add salt and pepper.

Break up noodles for soup and cook in boiling water 2 minutes. Discard flavor packet. Add rice and water chestnuts and stir.

Combine all ingredients and stir. Pour into large casserole sprayed with nonstick cooking spray; cover and bake for 1½–2 hours.

Recipe makes 10 servings.

Each serving provides:

219	Calories	2.1 g	Dietary fiber
4.6 g	Fat	273 mg	Sodium
9.7 g	Protein	28 mg	Cholesterol
21.2 g	Carbohydrates		

Orange Sweet Potato Casserole

4 medium sweet potatoes, baked
3 tablespoons orange juice concentrate
Grated peel from ½ orange
½ cup brown sugar
2 teaspoons lemon juice
2 teaspoons Molly McButter
2 cups miniature marshmallows

Preheat oven to 350 degrees F

Remove skin from baked sweet potatoes and place potatoes in large bowl. Add orange juice concentrate, grated orange peel, brown sugar, lemon juice, and Molly McButter and mix well. Fold in marshmallows. Place in casserole sprayed with nonstick cooking spray and bake for 25–35 minutes.

Recipe makes 6 servings.

Each serving provides:

216	Calories	2.4 g	Dietary fiber
0.1 g	Fat	83 mg	Sodium
1.8 g	Protein	0 mg	Cholesterol
53.3 g	Carbohydrates		

Onion Smothered Chicken

—❦—

2 boneless, skinless chicken breasts (3 ounces each)
¼ teaspoon garlic powder
¼ teaspoon onion powder
¼ teaspoon paprika
¼ cup fat-free chicken broth
1 clove garlic, pressed
1 large onion, sliced
2 green onions, chopped

Spray skillet with nonstick cooking spray. Season chicken breasts with garlic powder, onion powder, and paprika. Place in skillet and brown on each side. Add chicken broth to skillet and place garlic, regular onion, and green onion on top of chicken. Simmer with lid alternating off and on to cook everything thoroughly and to turn chicken a pretty golden brown.

Recipe makes 2 servings.

Each serving provides:

135	Calories	1.9 g	Dietary fiber
1.3 g	Fat	103 mg	Sodium
21.1 g	Protein	49 mg	Cholesterol
9 g	Carbohydrates		

Erma's Chicken with Curry Sauce

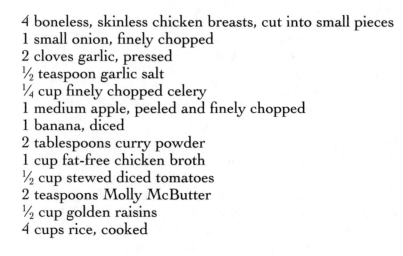

4 boneless, skinless chicken breasts, cut into small pieces
1 small onion, finely chopped
2 cloves garlic, pressed
½ teaspoon garlic salt
¼ cup finely chopped celery
1 medium apple, peeled and finely chopped
1 banana, diced
2 tablespoons curry powder
1 cup fat-free chicken broth
½ cup stewed diced tomatoes
2 teaspoons Molly McButter
½ cup golden raisins
4 cups rice, cooked

In large skillet sprayed with nonstick cooking spray, brown chicken pieces and onion. Add garlic and garlic salt and continue to brown. Add celery, apple, banana, and curry powder. Cook 1 minute. Add chicken broth, tomatoes, and Molly McButter. Stir and simmer over low heat 15 minutes. Add raisins for the last 5 minutes of cooking. Serve warm over rice.

Recipe makes 6 servings.

Each serving provides:

350	Calories	2.9 g	Dietary fiber
1.8 g	Fat	454 mg	Sodium
23.5 g	Protein	46 mg	Cholesterol
59.9 g	Carbohydrates		

Ranch Dinner

1 medium onion, chopped
1 large potato, peeled and cut into chunks (cooked in
    microwave until tender)
½ cup fat-free chicken broth
1 clove garlic, pressed
1 can (15 ounces) Ranch beans
1 can (10 ounces) Rotel tomatoes
½ cup 98 percent fat-free cream of mushroom soup
⅛ teaspoon onion powder
Salt and black pepper to taste

Spray large skillet with nonstick cooking spray. Add
onion and potato. Simmer and brown until potatoes are
done (30–35 minutes). Add chicken broth if necessary
while cooking to provide more moisture. Add remaining
ingredients and simmer 5–10 minutes.

Recipe makes 6 servings.

Each serving provides:

174	Calories	5.7 g	Dietary fiber
2.4 g	Fat	793 mg	Sodium
6.2 g	Protein	4 mg	Cholesterol
31.2 g	Carbohydrates		

Lite Reuben Sandwich

—❧—

1 medium onion, sliced
4 slices rye bread
Spicy hot mustard
½ pound lite ham, shaved
1 can (16 ounces) sauerkraut, well drained
4 slices fat-free Swiss cheese

In large skillet sprayed with nonstick cooking spray, brown and sauté onion.

Spread bread slices with mustard and place on cooking sheet sprayed with nonstick cooking spray. Place shaved ham on each bread slice, then spoon on sauerkraut. Top each with 1 slice cheese; spoon on onions. Place under broiler to melt cheese. Serve warm.

Recipe makes 4 servings.

Each serving provides:

203	Calories	4.6 g	Dietary fiber
2.1 g	Fat	1492 mg	Sodium
20 g	Protein	29 mg	Cholesterol
23.6 g	Carbohydrates		

Beef and Noodle Casserole

———— ✧ ————

1 package (8 ounces) medium lowfat (1 g fat) noodles
1 cup fat-free cottage cheese
1 carton (8 ounces) fat-free sour cream
½ cup chopped onion
½ cup chopped green pepper
1 pound lowfat ground beef
1 can (12 ounces) tomato paste
1 can (4 ounces) sliced mushrooms, undrained
1 teaspoon garlic powder
Black pepper to taste
1 cup shredded fat-free Cheddar or American cheese

Preheat oven to 350 degrees F

Cook noodles according to package directions and drain
well. Mix gently with cottage cheese, sour cream, onion,
and green pepper.

Brown ground beef in skillet, stirring to crumble,
and drain. Add tomato paste, mushrooms with liquid,
garlic powder, and pepper. Mix well and simmer
5 minutes, stirring occasionally.

Spoon half the noodle mixture into 9 × 13 inch baking dish sprayed with nonstick cooking spray; top with half the meat mixture, then repeat noodle layer and meat layer. Sprinkle top evenly with shredded cheese. Bake for 30 minutes or until cheese is melted and casserole is thoroughly heated.

Recipe makes 8 servings.

Each serving provides:

321	Calories	3.2 g	Dietary fiber
6.9 g	Fat	654 mg	Sodium
30.6 g	Protein	5 mg	Cholesterol
34.4 g	Carbohydrates		

Recipe Contributed by: Marilyn Stutsman, R.N.
Therapeutic Exercise Services
St. John Medical Center
Tulsa, Oklahoma

Chicken Breasts
with Wine Sauce

4 boneless, skinless chicken breasts
Onion powder to taste
Garlic powder to taste
Salt and black pepper to taste
2 tablespoons all-purpose flour

Sauce
1½ cups fat-free chicken broth
1 green onion, sliced
½ cup canned sliced mushrooms
2 tablespoons white cooking wine
1 teaspoon Molly McButter
2 tablespoons fat-free sour cream
1 tablespoon cornstarch
1 tablespoon very finely grated carrot for garnish

Spray large skillet with nonstick cooking spray. Season chicken breast with onion powder, garlic powder, salt, and pepper. Then dust with flour and place in skillet. Simmer chicken over medium-low heat until done and browned on both sides.

Remove chicken from skillet and stir in all ingredients for sauce except carrots. Save carrots for garnish. Stir with whisk until well blended. Continue to stir over medium heat until sauce starts to thicken. Pour sauce over chicken and serve.

Recipe makes 4 servings.

Each serving provides:

173	Calories	0.7 g	Dietary fiber
1.6 g	Fat	620 mg	Sodium
29.4 g	Protein	68 mg	Cholesterol
8 g	Carbohydrates		

Chicken-Fried Chicken with Cream Gravy

Chicken
4 boneless, skinless chicken breasts
2 egg whites, slightly beaten
2 cups cornflakes, crushed
Salt and black pepper to taste

Gravy
4 tablespoons flour
1 cup fat-free chicken broth
½ cup evaporated skim milk
1 cup skim milk
2 teaspoons Molly McButter
Salt and black pepper to taste

Lightly pound chicken breasts with table knife handle until they are thinner, larger, and lightly tenderized. Dip in egg white and roll in crushed cornflakes. In skillet sprayed with nonstick cooking spray, brown and cook over medium-low heat 5–6 minutes on each side (will burn easily; keep heat fairly low). Turn only once. When chicken is done, remove from skillet and add salt and pepper to taste.

Add flour to skillet and brown over medium heat, stirring occasionally. This will burn easily. Remove skillet from heat and set aside.

In medium bowl, combine remaining gravy ingredients. Using a whisk, with skillet still removed from heat, add gravy liquid to flour while stirring. Return to heat and whisk until gravy thickens. Serve gravy spooned over chicken.

Recipe makes 4 servings.

Each serving provides:

275	Calories	0.7 g	Dietary fiber
1.8 g	Fat	680 mg	Sodium
36.1 g	Protein	70 mg	Cholesterol
26.9 g	Carbohydrates		

Oven-Fried Chicken Breasts

———❦———

½ cup lowfat Pioneer Biscuit Mix*
2 tablespoons fat-free Parmesan cheese
½ teaspoon paprika
Garlic salt and black pepper to taste
4 boneless, skinless chicken breasts (3 ounces each)
⅓ cup fat-free liquid egg product

Preheat oven to 375 degrees F

In small bowl, mix together biscuit mix, Parmesan cheese, paprika, garlic salt, and black Pour into plastic bag.

*If you cannot find Pioneer lowfat biscuit mix in your supermarket, use another lowfat biscuit mix, which may be a few grams higher in fat.

Dip one chicken breast in liquid egg product, then shake in seasonings mixture. Repeat for all chicken breasts. Place on baking sheet sprayed with nonstick cooking spray and bake for 25–30 minutes, until done. Turn chicken over halfway through cooking.

Recipe makes 4 servings.

Each serving provides:

189	Calories	0.4 g	Dietary fiber
1.4 g	Fat	375 mg	Sodium
23.6 g	Protein	50 mg	Cholesterol
22 g	Carbohydrates		

Broccoli and Rice Casserole

—✿—

1 can (10¾ ounces) Campbell's 99 percent fat-free
    cream of chicken soup
2 teaspoons dry onion flakes
2 teaspoons Molly McButter
½ cup fat-free sour cream
1 package (2 ounces) dry ranch dressing mix
1 can (14 ounces) fat-free chicken broth
2 cups uncooked Minute Rice
1½ cups fresh broccoli, chopped or 1 box
    (10 ounces) frozen broccoli
½ cup grated fat-free American cheese
Black pepper to taste

Preheat oven to 350 degrees F

In large bowl, combine soup, onion flakes, Molly McButter, sour cream, dressing mix, and chicken broth. Beat with electric mixer until smooth. Add rice, broccoli, and cheese and stir with spoon. Add pepper. Pour into casserole sprayed with nonstick cooking spray; cover and bake for 40 minutes.

Recipe makes 8 servings.

Each serving provides:

161	Calories	0.8 g	Dietary fiber
0.8 g	Fat	1876 mg	Sodium
8.7 g	Protein	5 mg	Cholesterol
29.2 g	Carbohydrates		

Orange Shrimp

—❦—

½ cup fat-free chicken broth
¼ cup sweet orange marmalade
1 teaspoon lite soy sauce
4 green onions, chopped
1 teaspoon vinegar
1 clove garlic, pressed
2 teaspoons cornstarch
½ teaspoon Molly McButter
10 fresh jumbo shrimp, cooked, peeled, and deveined

In medium sauce pan combine all ingredients except shrimp. Stir over low heat until thickened. Add shrimp to sauce and heat long enough to warm shrimp through. Good served over rice.

Recipe makes 2 servings.

Each serving provides:

178	Calories	0.7 g	Dietary fiber
1.6 g	Fat	539 mg	Sodium
19.7 g	Protein	138 mg	Cholesterol
18.6 g	Carbohydrates		

Green Chile Rice

—❧—

1 can (10 ounces) green chile enchilada sauce
1 can (4 ounces) chopped green chilies
1 tablespoon dry onion flakes
2 teaspoons Molly McButter
1 teaspoon garlic salt
1 can (14 ounces) fat-free chicken broth
2 cups uncooked Minute Rice
½ cup shredded fat-free American cheese
Black pepper to taste

Preheat oven to 350 degrees F

In large bowl, combine enchilada sauce, green chilies, onion flakes, Molly McButter, garlic salt, and chicken broth. Add rice and shredded cheese and stir. Add pepper. Pour into casserole sprayed with nonstick cooking spray and bake uncovered for 40 minutes.

Recipe makes 8 servings.

Each serving provides:

126	Calories	0.5 g	Dietary fiber
1 g	Fat	733 mg	Sodium
4.7 g	Protein	1 mg	Cholesterol
24.1 g	Carbohydrates		

Taco Tamale Pie

———— ✤ ————

⅓ pound extra lean ground beef
1 small onion, chopped
1 clove garlic, pressed
½ cup diced canned tomatoes
2 teaspoons taco seasoning
1 cup canned or frozen corn
½ cup cornmeal
⅓ cup fat-free liquid egg product
1 cup milk
¼ cup Sargento light grated Cheddar cheese

Preheat oven to 350 degrees F

Brown ground beef and onion in skillet. Add garlic and
continue browning. Add tomatoes, taco seasoning,
and corn. Simmer for 2 minutes.

In medium bowl, combine cornmeal, egg product, and milk and stir.

Spray 9 × 9 inch baking dish with nonstick cooking spray. Pour meat mixture into baking dish and spread evenly. Pour cornmeal mixture over top and sprinkle on cheese. Bake for 25–30 minutes.

Recipe makes 4 servings.

Each serving provides:

255	Calories	3.9 g	Dietary fiber
5.8 g	Fat	835 mg	Sodium
18.1 g	Protein	25 mg	Cholesterol
34.1 g	Carbohydrates		

Chicken Breasts with Apricot–Orange Sauce

4 boneless, skinless chicken breasts
½ teaspoon garlic powder
½ teaspoon onion powder
Salt and black pepper to taste
¾ cup fat-free chicken broth
2 teaspoons cornstarch
2 tablespoons frozen orange juice concentrate
¼ cup apricot preserves
2 teaspoons lite soy sauce
2 green onions, chopped

Spray skillet with nonstick cooking spray. Season both sides of each chicken breast with garlic powder, onion powder, salt, and pepper. Brown and simmer chicken breasts over low-medium heat until done.

Remove cooked chicken from skillet. Stir in chicken broth, cornstarch, orange juice, apricot preserves, soy sauce, and green onions. Simmer sauce and stir until thickened. Return chicken to pan, turning to coat. Cover and simmer 5 minutes.

Recipe makes 4 servings.

Each serving provides:

214	Calories	0.5 g	Dietary fiber
1.5 g	Fat	571 mg	Sodium
28.6 g	Protein	68 mg	Cholesterol
20.3 g	Carbohydrates		

Tabasco Chicken

———∽✢∾———

4 boneless, skinless chicken breasts
Tabasco sauce
Garlic salt
Onion powder
Black pepper

Rinse and pat dry chicken breasts. Generously shake
Tabasco sauce on each side, then season each side with
garlic salt, onion powder, and black pepper.

Brown and simmer in skillet sprayed with nonstick
cooking spray until done and tender. Serve.

Recipe makes 4 servings.

Each serving provides:

129	Calories	0 g	Dietary fiber
1.5 g	Fat	76 mg	Sodium
27.2 g	Protein	68 mg	Cholesterol
0 g	Carbohydrates		

French Onion Chicken and Potato Bake

4 boneless, skinless chicken breasts
Garlic powder
Black pepper
2 potatoes, peeled and cut into chunks
1 can (10½ ounces) Campbell's French onion soup

Preheat oven to 350 degrees F

Season both sides of chicken breasts with garlic powder and pepper. Brown in skillet sprayed with nonstick cooking spray. Place in 8-inch baking dish sprayed with nonstick cooking spray.

Cover chicken with potato chunks. Pour soup over top and sprinkle with black pepper. Cover and bake for 40–50 minutes or until potatoes are done.

Recipe makes 4 servings.

Each serving provides:

274	Calories	2.7 g	Dietary fiber
2.6 g	Fat	725 mg	Sodium
31.8 g	Protein	68 mg	Cholesterol
30.5 g	Carbohydrates		

Barbecue Chicken and Coleslaw Sandwich

1 pound boneless, skinless chicken breasts
1 cup barbecue sauce
2 teaspoons dry onion flakes
6 lite hamburger buns
⅓ cup buttermilk coleslaw for each sandwich
    (see page 77)

Brown chicken in skillet sprayed with nonstick cooking spray. Cover and simmer until tender. Remove from skillet and cool until easily handled.

Cut chicken into about 2-inch pieces and shred with fingers or chop into small pieces. Return to skillet and cover with barbecue sauce. Add onion flakes. Stir and simmer over low heat.

Place a few spoonfuls of meat on each hamburger bun and top with scoop of coleslaw. Place top of bun on sandwich and enjoy.

Recipe makes 6 servings. (Nutritional figures do not include coleslaw.)

Each serving provides:

301	Calories	1.7 g	Dietary fiber
3.1 g	Fat	748 mg	Sodium
23.4 g	Protein	44 mg	Cholesterol
44.4 g	Carbohydrates		

Pimiento Chicken

4 boneless, skinless chicken breasts
$\frac{1}{2}$ teaspoon garlic salt
Black pepper to taste
1 cup (8 ounces) Kraft fat-free cream cheese
1 jar (4 ounces) chopped pimientos
2 teaspoons dry onion flakes
$\frac{1}{4}$ cup fat-free chicken broth
$\frac{1}{2}$ green pepper, chopped

Preheat oven to 350 degrees F

Brown chicken breasts in skillet sprayed with nonstick cooking spray. While cooking, season with garlic salt and pepper.

In medium bowl, combine cream cheese, pimientos, onion flakes, chicken broth, and green pepper. Stir until well blended.

Place chicken breasts in casserole sprayed with nonstick cooking spray. Pour cream cheese mixture over top and bake for 35 minutes.

Recipe makes 4 servings.

Each serving provides:

193	Calories	0.8 g	Dietary fiber
1.6 g	Fat	669 mg	Sodium
35.9 g	Protein	77 mg	Cholesterol
7 g	Carbohydrates		

Honey Dijon Oven Chicken

½ cup honey
¼ cup Dijon mustard
1 clove garlic, pressed
1 small onion, finely chopped
4 boneless, skinless chicken breasts
2 cups crushed cornflakes
Salt and black pepper to taste

Preheat oven to 350 degrees F

In small bowl, combine honey, mustard, garlic, and onion.

Dip chicken breasts in mixture and roll in cornflakes. Place on baking sheet sprayed with nonstick cooking spray and sprinkle with salt and pepper. Discard any remaining honey mustard mixture when finished. Bake for 30–35 minutes.

Recipe makes 4 servings.

Each serving provides:

342	Calories	1.1 g	Dietary fiber
2.6 g	Fat	643 mg	Sodium
29.8 g	Protein	68 mg	Cholesterol
50.6 g	Carbohydrates		

Savory Apricot Chicken

—❦—

4 boneless, skinless chicken breasts
½ package dry Lipton onion soup mix
½ package dry Lipton savory herb and garlic soup mix
1 jar (12 ounces) apricot preserves
½ cup fat-free chicken broth

Preheat oven to 350 degrees F

Place chicken breasts in baking dish sprayed with non-stick cooking spray. Combine remaining ingredients and mix well. Pour over chicken and bake uncovered for 45–50 minutes.

Recipe makes 4 servings.

Each serving provides:

420	Calories	0.9 g	Dietary fiber
2 g	Fat	1564 mg	Sodium
30.1 g	Protein	69 mg	Cholesterol
71.1 g	Carbohydrates		

Jalapeño Chicken

———❧———

1 pound boneless, skinless chicken breasts
½ teaspoon Molly McButter
1 jar (8 or 10 ounces) jalapeño jelly
⅓ cup fat-free chicken broth
1 package (4.3 ounces) dry Lipton onion soup mix
4 cups rice, cooked

Preheat oven to 350 degrees F

Place chicken breasts in 8-inch baking dish sprayed with nonstick cooking spray and sprinkle with Molly McButter.

In medium bowl, combine and stir together jalapeño jelly, chicken broth, and onion soup mix. Pour over chicken and bake for 45 minutes. Serve over rice.

Recipe makes 4 servings.

Each serving provides:

622	Calories	1.8 g	Dietary fiber
3.8 g	Fat	2934 mg	Sodium
35.4 g	Protein	67 mg	Cholesterol
110.7 g	Carbohydrates		

Clam Linguine

—✥—

½ cup evaporated skim milk
1½ cups skim milk
2 cans (6 ounces each) minced clams with liquid
½ small onion, chopped
1 clove garlic, pressed
¼ cup fat-free sour cream
¼ cup fat-free Parmesan cheese
2 teaspoons Molly McButter
½ teaspoon parsley
Salt and black pepper to taste
1 tablespoon cornstarch (optional)
4 cups cooked linguine noodles

In large saucepan, combine all ingredients except cornstarch and noodles. Simmer and stir over medium-low heat 5–10 minutes. Use cornstarch to thicken if desired. Serve over noodles.

Recipe makes 4 servings.

Each serving provides:

372	Calories	2.6 g	Dietary fiber
2.2 g	Fat	892 mg	Sodium
27.1 g	Protein	43 mg	Cholesterol
58.9 g	Carbohydrates		

Noodle Casserole

———❦———

1 package (12 ounces) No Yolk noodles
½ teaspoon Molly McButter
1 pound ground turkey breast or chicken breast
1 small onion, chopped
1 can (6 ounces) tomato paste
⅓ cup fat-free chicken broth
¼ teaspoon garlic powder
½ teaspoon Worcestershire sauce
Salt and black pepper to taste
1½ cups fat-free cottage cheese
1 cup (8 ounces) Kraft fat-free cream cheese
⅓ cup fat-free sour cream

Preheat oven to 350 degrees F

Cook noodles according to package directions; rinse, drain, and sprinkle with Molly McButter.

Brown meat and onion in skillet sprayed with nonstick cooking spray. Add tomato paste, chicken broth, garlic powder, Worcestershire sauce, salt, and pepper. Remove from heat and set aside to cool.

In large bowl, combine cottage cheese, cream cheese, and sour cream. Stir with spoon until well blended. Add meat mixture and stir. Fold in noodles. Pour mixture into large casserole sprayed with nonstick cooking spray; cover and bake for 35–40 minutes.

Recipe makes 8 servings.

Each serving provides:

304	Calories	2.4 g	Dietary fiber
1.9 g	Fat	569 mg	Sodium
31 g	Protein	43 mg	Cholesterol
39.8 g	Carbohydrates		

Rotel Chicken
with Sour Cream

———◦✻◦———

4 boneless, skinless chicken breasts (3 ounces each)
¼ teaspoon garlic powder
¼ teaspoon onion powder
½ teaspoon chili powder
Salt and black pepper to taste
¼ cup 98 percent fat-free condensed
    cream of chicken soup
1 can (10¾ ounces) 98 percent fat-free condensed
    cream of mushroom soup
¼ cup fat-free sour cream
1 small onion, chopped
½ cup canned Rotel tomatoes
½ cup fat-free evaporated milk
4 small soft corn tortillas
½ cup Sargento light grated Cheddar cheese

Preheat oven to 350 degrees F

Season chicken breasts with garlic powder, onion powder, chili powder, salt, and pepper. Brown on each side in a skillet sprayed with nonstick cooking spray.

In large bowl, combine soups, sour cream, onion, Rotel tomatoes, evaporated milk, and onion. Mix with a whisk until well blended.

Spray 9 × 9 inch glass baking dish with nonstick cooking spray. Place corn tortillas on bottom and up the sides of dish. Place chicken breasts in dish and pour soup mixture over chicken. Bake for 35–40 minutes. Sprinkle with grated cheese last 15 minutes of cooking time.

Recipe makes 4 servings.

Each serving provides:

303	Calories	2.5 g	Dietary fiber
5.7 g	Fat	737 mg	Sodium
30.3 g	Protein	60 mg	Cholesterol
31.5 g	Carbohydrates		

Onion-Mushroom Meat Loaf

2 pounds ground turkey breast or chicken breast
1 package (4.3 ounces) dry Lipton onion-mushroom
    soup mix
2 egg whites, slightly beaten
½ cup fat-free sour cream
¼ teaspoon black pepper
¼ teaspoon garlic powder

Preheat oven to 350 degrees F

In large bowl, combine all ingredients until well mixed.
Pour into loaf pan or dish sprayed with nonstick cooking
spray and bake for 1 hour and 20 minutes. Remove and
serve. Wonderful served with baked potato.

Recipe makes 8 servings.

Each serving provides:

191	Calories	0 g	Dietary fiber
2.5 g	Fat	1068 mg	Sodium
30.3 g	Protein	68 mg	Cholesterol
1.7 g	Carbohydrates		

Lemon Garlic Pasta

———— ✖ ————

1 package (½ ounce) Butter Buds
⅔ cup hot water
1 tablespoon Molly McButter
2½ tablespoons fresh lemon juice
2 cloves garlic, pressed
3 cups cooked spaghetti or linguini
Chopped parsley for garnish (optional)
Garlic salt to taste

In small pan, mix Butter Buds with hot water and Molly McButter. Add lemon juice and garlic. Stir over low heat for 3–5 minutes. Just simmer—do not boil.

Pour over hot cooked pasta and toss. Add chopped parsley and garlic salt to taste, if desired.

Recipe makes 3 servings.

Each serving provides:

222	Calories	2.3 g	Dietary fiber
1.1 g	Fat	429 mg	Sodium
6.9 g	Protein	0 mg	Cholesterol
45.8 g	Carbohydrates		

Focaccia with Roasted Garlic and Onion

Dough
2 teaspoons dry yeast
2 teaspoons sugar
1 teaspoon salt
½ cup dry instant potato flakes
1½ teaspoons Molly McButter
4½ cups all-purpose flour
2½ cups warm water (115 degrees F)
2 teaspoons olive oil

Topping
1 large sweet onion, thinly sliced
6 whole cloves of fresh garlic, slivered
1–2 tablespoons white cooking wine
Garlic salt to taste

Preheat oven to 375 degrees F

In large bowl, combine yeast, sugar, salt, potato flakes, Molly McButter, and flour. Stir well.

Add warm water and oil to flour mixture, mixing thoroughly. Cover bowl tightly and place in warm spot to rise. Let sit until it doubles, about 1 hour.

While dough is rising, spray skillet with nonstick cooking spray. Sauté onion and garlic slivers slowly over low heat for 5–8 minutes. Add 1 tablespoon of white wine to skillet if moisture is needed. Remove from heat.

Spray large baking pan (or large pizza pan) with nonstick cooking spray.

When dough has doubled, turn it out onto prepared pan. Press to fit pan, and top with onion, garlic, and garlic salt.

Bake for 45 minutes until done. Cut with pizza cutter. Serve with soups or pasta or as an appetizer with garlic dip.

Recipe makes 10 servings.

Each serving provides:

242	Calories	2.3 g	Dietary fiber
1.6 g	Fat	252 mg	Sodium
6.9 g	Protein	0 mg	Cholesterol
48.9 g	Carbohydrates		

Quick and Easy
Chicken Kebabs

—⚬✖⚬—

Pineapple juice (reserved from chunks below)
⅓ cup lite soy sauce
1 clove garlic, pressed
½ teaspoon sesame seeds
2 boneless, skinless chicken breasts cut into chunks
    (3 ounces each)
1 medium onion cut into chunks
1 green or red bell pepper, cut into chunks
1 can (8 ounces) pineapple chunks (save juice)

In medium bowl, combine pineapple juice, soy sauce, garlic, and sesame seeds.

Place chicken in zipper plastic bag and add half the marinade to bag.

Place onion, bell pepper, and pineapple in another bag and add remaining marinade. Marinate all for at least an hour.

Using skewers, alternate meat, veggies, and pineapple on each skewer. Cook over charcoal grill or in oven broiler. Cook 2–3 minutes and rotate. Repeat procedure.

Recipe makes 6 servings.

Each serving provides:

83	Calories	1.3 g	Dietary fiber
0.6 g	Fat	558 mg	Sodium
8.1 g	Protein	16 mg	Cholesterol
11.2 g	Carbohydrates		

Onion Cheese Pie

—— ❧ ——

2 large fat-free flour tortillas
Buttermist nonstick cooking spray
1 teaspoon Molly McButter
1 carton (16 ounces) fat-free cottage cheese
$\frac{1}{3}$ cup fat-free liquid egg product
2 teaspoons dry onion flakes
1 medium onion, thinly sliced
$\frac{1}{3}$ cup fat-free Parmesan cheese
5 slices fat-free Swiss cheese
$\frac{1}{3}$ cup grated fat-free Cheddar cheese
1 large ripe tomato, thinly sliced
Garlic salt
Black pepper to taste

Preheat oven to 325 degrees F

Place 1 tortilla in a large pie plate sprayed with nonstick cooking spray. Spray tortilla lightly with Buttermist and sprinkle with $\frac{1}{2}$ teaspoon Molly McButter. Repeat process with second tortilla on top of the other.

In a large bowl, combine cottage cheese, egg product, and onion flakes and mix with spoon. Pour half over tortillas and gently smooth and spread with spoon.

Add layers in this order: half of the sliced onion, all the Parmesan and Swiss cheese, the remaining cottage cheese mixture, all the Cheddar cheese, the remaining sliced onion, and all the sliced tomato. Sprinkle top with garlic salt and pepper.

Bake for 1 hour and 20 minutes. Cool slightly before slicing.

Recipe makes 8 servings.

Each serving provides:

141	Calories	1.9 g	Dietary fiber
0.5 g	Fat	446 mg	Sodium
17.2 g	Protein	10 mg	Cholesterol
15.5 g	Carbohydrates		

Parmesan Noodles

———— ✦ ————

1 package (12 ounces) No Yolk noodles
1 tablespoon plus 2 teaspoons Molly McButter added to
    water to boil noodles
Nonfat butter-flavored nonstick cooking spray
¼ cup fat-free Parmesan cheese
Black pepper to taste

Prepare noodles according to package directions. I like
to use about 1 tablespoon Molly McButter in water
when boiling noodles. Drain and rinse noodles, draining
only slightly to leave some moisture to help melt cheese
and dissolve Molly McButter.

    Spray noodles lightly with nonstick cooking spray
and toss. Sprinkle with 2 teaspoons Molly McButter and
Parmesan and toss. Add pepper to taste and toss. Serve
immediately.

Recipe makes 4 servings.

Each serving provides:

326	Calories	2.3 g	Dietary fiber
1.7 g	Fat	245 mg	Sodium
13 g	Protein	3 mg	Cholesterol
62.3 g	Carbohydrates		

Oven Crispy
Onion–Mushroom Chicken

¾ cup Kraft fat-free mayonnaise
1 tablespoon dry Lipton onion-mushroom soup mix
4 boneless, skinless chicken breasts
3–4 cups cornflakes, crushed
Salt and black pepper to taste

Preheat oven to 350 degrees F

Combine mayonnaise and dry soup mix; let stand
5–10 minutes so onion flakes will soften.
　　If chicken breasts are wet, pat dry. Dip chicken
breasts in mayonnaise mixture, roll in cornflake crumbs,
and place in pan or cookie sheet sprayed with nonstick
cooking spray. Season with salt and pepper. Bake for
30–35 minutes.

Recipe makes 4 servings.

Each serving provides:

251	Calories	0.8 g	Dietary fiber
1.6 g	Fat	998 mg	Sodium
29.1 g	Protein	68 mg	Cholesterol
29.1 g	Carbohydrates		

Honey Crunchy Chicken

—✄—

¼ cup honey plus a little more for garnish
½ cup Kraft fat-free mayonnaise
¼–½ teaspoon blackened or Cajun spices (to taste)
Salt and black pepper to taste
4 boneless, skinless chicken breasts
1½ cups Grape Nuts cereal

In small bowl, mix honey, mayonnaise, and spices. Pour into container large enough to dip chicken breasts. Use another container large enough to roll dipped chicken in Grape Nuts.

Dip chicken breasts in honey mixture, then roll in Grape Nuts until covered. Place in skillet sprayed with nonstick cooking spray. Drizzle about 1 teaspoon honey over each chicken breast.

Cover and simmer 15 minutes on medium-low heat. Turn and cook additional 15 minutes. Drizzle honey on again after turning. Try not to turn more than once, as this disturbs coating. Be sure chicken is covered during cooking.

Recipe makes 4 servings.

Each serving provides:

396	Calories	3.8 g	Dietary fiber
2.2 g	Fat	770 mg	Sodium
32.3 g	Protein	68 mg	Cholesterol
61.7 g	Carbohydrates		

Crispy Honey Dijon Chicken

¾ cup Kraft fat-free mayonnaise
1 tablespoon dry Hidden Valley Honey Dijon
      Salad Dressing mix
4 boneless, skinless chicken breasts
¾ cup Kellogg's Apple Raisin Crisp cereal, crushed
Salt and black pepper to taste
1 package (12 ounces) No Yolk noodles (optional)

Preheat oven to 350 degrees F

Mix together mayonnaise and dry salad dressing mix.
If there is any moisture on chicken breasts, pat dry.
Dip chicken in mayonnaise mixture and roll in
crushed cereal.

Place on cookie sheet or pan sprayed with nonstick cooking spray. Season with salt and pepper. Bake for 30–35 minutes.

If desired, prepare noodles according to package directions while chicken is baking. Serve chicken breasts on bed of noodles.

Recipe makes 4 servings.

Each serving provides:

187	Calories	0.4 g	Dietary fiber
1.5 g	Fat	917 mg	Sodium
27.9 g	Protein	68 mg	Cholesterol
14 g	Carbohydrates		

Creole Gravy Chicken with Rice

Chicken
4 boneless, skinless chicken breasts
Garlic powder to taste
Black pepper to taste
1 package (4.3 ounces) Lipton rice and sauce mix,
    mushroom flavor
2 cups fat-free chicken broth
2 teaspoons Molly McButter

Creole Gravy
¼ cup fat-free chicken broth
⅛ cup evaporated skim milk
½ cup fat-free sour cream
4 tablespoons spicy brown mustard
¼ teaspoon blackened or Cajun spices
1½ teaspoons sugar
1 teaspoon Molly McButter

Preheat oven to 350 degrees F

Season chicken breasts with garlic powder and pepper.
Brown on both sides in skillet sprayed with nonstick
cooking spray.

Sprinkle rice and sauce mix evenly over bottom of 8- or 9-inch square baking dish sprayed with nonstick cooking spray. Add chicken broth. Sprinkle Molly McButter over top. Place chicken breasts over mixture and bake uncovered for 30–35 minutes or until most of the juice has been absorbed by the rice.

While chicken and rice are cooking, prepare Creole gravy. In small saucepan, combine all ingredients and stir over low heat.

Pour Creole gravy over each chicken breast just before serving.

Recipe makes 4 servings.

Each serving provides:

321	Calories	0.7 g	Dietary fiber
3.2 g	Fat	1540 mg	Sodium
34.9 g	Protein	68 mg	Cholesterol
33.5 g	Carbohydrates		

Chili Dogs in a Blanket

———✦———

6 fat-free hot dogs
6 teaspoons prepared mustard (or to taste)
3 teaspoons dry Lipton onion soup mix
3 teaspoons dry ranch dressing mix
6 teaspoons Williams Chili Makin's (in jar)
2½ cups Pioneer Low-Fat Biscuit Mix*
1 cup evaporated skim milk

Preheat oven to 350 degrees F

Slice each hot dog lengthwise (do not cut all the way through). Squirt a strip of mustard down center of split.

Add ½ teaspoon onion soup mix and ½ teaspoon dressing mix in each split on top of mustard. Add 1 teaspoon Chili Makin's on each. Set stuffed hot dogs aside.

Combine biscuit mix and evaporated milk and mix thoroughly. Dough will be stiff.

*If you can't find Pioneer Low-Fat Biscuit Mix in your area, use a light biscuit mix; however, this substitution will add a few grams of fat to each serving.

Spray large dinner plate with nonstick cooking spray and spray your hands lightly. Using your hands, roll about ½ cup dough into ball. Use your fingers to flatten ball of dough on plate until about the size of a small tortilla. Place a stuffed hot dog across center of dough. Wrap dough around hot dog and pinch to seal. Repeat for each hot dog.

Place in 9 × 13 inch casserole sprayed with nonstick cooking spray, leaving space between each for dough to expand. Bake for 25 minutes or until golden brown.

Recipe makes 6 servings.

Each serving provides:

345	Calories	1.2 g	Dietary fiber
1.2 g	Fat	1752 mg	Sodium
13.9 g	Protein	17 mg	Cholesterol
78.5 g	Carbohydrates		

Corn Quiche

—❧—

½ cup fat-free liquid egg product
¾ cup Pioneer Low-Fat Biscuit Mix*
1 cup fat-free cottage cheese
½ cup fat-free sour cream
2 teaspoons Molly McButter
1 can (16 ounces) whole-kernel corn, drained
2 teaspoons dry onion flakes
½ cup grated fat-free cheese

Preheat oven to 350 degrees F

Combine egg product, biscuit mix, cottage cheese, sour cream, and Molly McButter and beat with electric mixer about 2 minutes.

With spoon, fold in corn, onion flakes, and grated cheese and mix thoroughly. Pour into 10-inch pie plate sprayed with nonstick cooking spray and bake for 30–35 minutes.

Recipe makes 6 servings.

Each serving provides:

173	Calories	1.1 g	Dietary fiber
0.7 g	Fat	636 mg	Sodium
13.9 g	Protein	5 mg	Cholesterol
32.4 g	Carbohydrates		

---

*If you can't find Pioneer Low-Fat Biscuit Mix in your area, use a light biscuit mix; however, this substitution will add a few grams of fat to each serving.

Breakfast Burrito

½ teaspoon dry onion flakes
½ cup fat-free liquid egg product
1 slice turkey bacon, cooked and crumbled
1 slice Kraft fat-free American cheese,
    torn into small pieces
1 tablespoon chopped green chilies
Salt and black pepper to taste
Dash of Tabasco sauce (optional)
2 teaspoons fat-free sour cream
1 small fat-free flour tortilla

Add onion flakes to egg product and set aside 5–10 minutes for onion flakes to soften.

In small bowl, combine all ingredients except sour cream and tortilla. Scramble mixture in skillet sprayed with nonstick cooking spray over medium-low heat. Cheese will burn if heat is too high.

When egg mixture is almost done, stir in sour cream. Place on tortilla and roll up. Enjoy.

Recipe makes 1 serving.

Each serving provides:

190	Calories	2.5 g	Dietary fiber
2.1 g	Fat	744 mg	Sodium
22.1 g	Protein	10 mg	Cholesterol
20.8 g	Carbohydrates		

Chicken Gumbo

1 pound boneless, skinless chicken breasts, cut into
  small pieces
1 slice turkey bacon
¼ –½ teaspoon Cajun or blackened spices
  (more is better)
1 can (14½ ounces) stewed tomatoes
1 can (14 ounces) fat-free chicken broth
2 teaspoons dry onion flakes
½ cup frozen cut okra
1 stalk celery, chopped
2 tablespoons chopped green pepper
⅛ teaspoon garlic powder or salt
2 cups water
¾ cup instant rice
1 tablespoon dry ranch dressing mix
Salt and black pepper to taste
Dash of seasoned salt

In large pot sprayed with nonstick cooking spray, brown chicken pieces with turkey bacon. Season with Cajun or blackened spices while browning. Add remaining ingredients and simmer until rice is done.

Recipe makes 6 servings.

Each serving provides:

224	Calories	1.2 g	Dietary fiber
1.9 g	Fat	1572 mg	Sodium
31.6 g	Protein	70 mg	Cholesterol
19.1 g	Carbohydrates		

Spinach and Carrot Quiche

—⚬—

1 9-inch frozen regular Pet Ritz pie crust
1¼ cups fat-free liquid egg product
1 cup chopped fresh spinach
2 green onions, chopped
⅓ cup fat-free sour cream
1 teaspoon Molly McButter
¼ cup grated raw carrot
½ cup canned sliced mushrooms
Salt and black pepper to taste
¼ cup Sargento light grated Cheddar cheese

Preheat oven to 350 degrees F

While pie crust is still frozen, remove from aluminum pie plate and place in glass pie plate.

In large bowl, combine all remaining ingredients except cheese. Mix thoroughly and pour into unbaked pie shell. Sprinkle top with grated cheese and bake for about 40 minutes or until set.

Recipe makes 6 servings.

Each serving provides:

161	Calories	0.8 g	Dietary fiber
6.3 g	Fat	321 mg	Sodium
9.2 g	Protein	6 mg	Cholesterol
16.2 g	Carbohydrates		

Stuffed Bell Peppers

4 medium bell peppers
1 pound ground chicken breast or turkey breast
½ can (10¾ ounces) Campbell's 98 percent fat-free
    cream of mushroom soup
½ cup uncooked rice
2 egg whites
1 tablespoon dry onion flakes
½ teaspoon garlic powder
½ teaspoon salt (optional)
½ teaspoon black pepper

Preheat oven to 375 degrees F

Cut tops off bell peppers and remove seeds. Set aside.
    In large bowl, combine remaining ingredients
and mix well. Fill peppers with mixture and bake in
baking dish sprayed with nonstick cooking spray for
40–50 minutes.

Recipe makes 4 servings.

Each serving provides:

266	Calories	1.9 g	Dietary fiber
2.4 g	Fat	266 mg	Sodium
30.8 g	Protein	67 mg	Cholesterol
28.7 g	Carbohydrates		

Mexican Burgers

———— ✧ ————

1 pound ground turkey breast or chicken breast
½ cup chopped onion
¼ cup chopped green chilies
1 clove garlic, pressed or ½ teaspoon garlic powder
½ teaspoon chili powder
½ teaspoon Tabasco sauce
Salt and black pepper to taste

Combine all ingredients and mix thoroughly. Shape into patties and cook in large skillet sprayed with nonstick cooking spray.

    Makes 4–6 burgers, depending on size and thickness desired. Serve on lite hamburger buns.

Recipe makes 6 servings.

Each serving provides:

96	Calories	0.4 g	Dietary fiber
1.3 g	Fat	52 mg	Sodium
18 g	Protein	45 mg	Cholesterol
2.1 g	Carbohydrates		

Philly Turkey with Swiss on a Bagel

4–5 thin strips green pepper
½ small onion, sliced
2–4 tablespoons fat-free Italian salad dressing
1 large plain bagel, cut in half horizontally
3 ounces shaved turkey luncheon meat
1 slice Bordens' fat-free Swiss cheese

Add peppers and onions to skillet sprayed with nonstick cooking spray and stir over medium heat. Add 2 tablespoons Italian dressing and continue to stir until peppers and onions are tender.

Pour a little Italian dressing on each bagel half. Top with turkey and add peppers and onions. Place cheese on next and place top on sandwich. Warm in microwave oven 1 minute to melt cheese; serve warm.

Recipe makes 1 serving.

Each serving provides:

473	Calories	3.8 g	Dietary fiber
3.5 g	Fat	1894 mg	Sodium
36.5 g	Protein	23 mg	Cholesterol
72.5 g	Carbohydrates		

Tuna Lasagna

———⊰❦⊱———

1 can (10¾ ounces) Campbell's 98 percent fat-free
    cream of mushroom soup
⅓ cup fat-free sour cream
1 cup fat-free chicken broth
2 cans (6⅛ ounces each) water-packed tuna
2 teaspoons dry onion flakes
1 can (4 ounces) sliced mushrooms, drained
Black pepper to taste
1½ cups fat-free cottage cheese
½ cup fat-free liquid egg product
1 package (8 ounces) lasagna noodles,
    cooked and drained
1 cup shredded fat-free mozzarella cheese
⅓ cup fat-free Parmesan cheese
1 teaspoon garlic salt

Preheat oven to 350 degrees F

In large bowl, stir together soup, sour cream, chicken broth, tuna, onion flakes, and mushrooms. Mix thoroughly. Add pepper and mix.

In small bowl, combine cottage cheese and egg product.

In large baking dish sprayed with nonstick cooking spray, layer half each of the noodles, mozzarella, tuna mixture, Parmesan, cottage cheese mixture, and garlic salt. Repeat layers. Bake for 35–40 minutes.

Recipe makes 8 servings.

Each serving provides:

257	Calories	1.3 g	Dietary fiber
1.6 g	Fat	1055 mg	Sodium
27.9 g	Protein	22 mg	Cholesterol
30.6 g	Carbohydrates		

Old-Fashioned Homestyle Noodles

2 cups water
1 can (14 ounces) fat-free chicken broth
1 package (12 ounces) Reames Free frozen
   home-style noodles
1 stalk celery, chopped
1 tablespoon dry onion flakes
1 can (10¾ ounces) Campbell's 98 percent fat-free
   cream of chicken soup
1 cup skim milk
1½ tablespoons Molly McButter
Salt and black pepper to taste
1 package (10 ounces) frozen peas
½ cup fat-free sour cream

Bring water and chicken broth to boil in large kettle. Add noodles, celery, and onion flakes and simmer 20 minutes.

Add remaining ingredients except peas and sour cream. Simmer 2 minutes. Add peas and sour cream; simmer 3–4 minutes. **Do not boil.** Serve.

Recipe makes 6 servings.

Each serving provides:

266	Calories	3.8 g	Dietary fiber
1.8 g	Fat	770 mg	Sodium
12 g	Protein	5 mg	Cholesterol
49.2g	Carbohydrates		

Tortilla Casserole

—✎—

Nonfat butter-flavored nonstick cooking spray
2 small onions, chopped
1 can (16 ounces) fat-free refried beans
1 pound ground turkey breast
1 package (1¼ ounces) taco seasoning
½ cup water
1 can (10¾ ounces) Campbell's 98 percent fat-free
    cream of mushroom soup
1 can (4 ounces) chopped green chilies
½ cup fat-free sour cream
½ cup grated fat-free Cheddar cheese
1 cup crushed no-oil tortilla chips

Preheat oven to 350 degrees F

Spray 9 × 13 casserole with cooking spray. Combine
1 chopped onion with refried beans and line bottom of
casserole with mixture.

Brown meat in skillet sprayed with nonstick cooking spray. Add taco seasoning and stir. Add water and stir. Add cream of mushroom soup and green chilies; remove from heat. Add sour cream and mix thoroughly.

Pour mixture over refried beans. Add second chopped onion. Sprinkle on grated cheese and top with tortilla chips. Bake for 25–35 minutes.

Recipe makes 9 servings.

Each serving provides:

210	Calories	4.6 g	Dietary fiber
1.9 g	Fat	781 mg	Sodium
19.5 g	Protein	33 mg	Cholesterol
29.9 g	Carbohydrates		

Cauliflower and Broccoli Stir-Fry

1½ cups cauliflower pieces
1½ cups broccoli pieces
3 green onions, chopped
1 cup (¼ pound) fresh mushrooms, sliced
Salt to taste
¾ cup fat-free Italian dressing
2 teaspoons grated orange peel

In large skillet sprayed with nonstick cooking spray, stir-fry cauliflower, broccoli, onions, and mushrooms over medium heat 4–5 minutes. Add small amount of water (¼ to ½ cup); cover and simmer 1–2 minutes. Remove lid and cook until most of the liquid is absorbed. Add salt, dressing, and orange peel and stir. Serve immediately.

Recipe makes 2 servings.

Each serving provides:

83	Calories	4 g	Dietary fiber
0.5 g	Fat	212 mg	Sodium
4.2 g	Protein	0 mg	Cholesterol
18.9 g	Carbohydrates		

Crispy Buttermilk Chicken

¾ cup lowfat buttermilk
½ teaspoon garlic salt
2 cloves garlic, pressed
Black pepper to taste
4 boneless, skinless chicken breasts
2 cups cornflakes, crushed

Preheat oven to 350 degrees F

Mix together buttermilk, garlic salt, garlic, and pepper.
Dip chicken breasts in mixture and roll in cornflakes.
Bake on baking sheet sprayed with nonstick cooking
spray for 25–35 minutes.

Recipe makes 4 servings.

Each serving provides:

205	Calories	0.5 g	Dietary fiber
1.9 g	Fat	545 mg	Sodium
30 g	Protein	70 mg	Cholesterol
15.8 g	Carbohydrates		

Vegetable Fajitas

—❧—

1 teaspoon sesame seeds
1 large onion, sliced
1 bell pepper, sliced
1 small zucchini, sliced
1 small yellow squash, sliced
3 fresh green chilies, sliced lengthwise
1 cup ($\frac{1}{4}$ pound) mushrooms, sliced
2 teaspoons dry fajita seasoning
1 teaspoon garlic salt
Black pepper to taste
$\frac{1}{2}$ cup shredded fat-free Cheddar cheese
6 small flour tortillas
Salsa (optional)

In large skillet sprayed with nonstick cooking spray, lightly brown sesame seeds. Add onion and brown. Add bell pepper, zucchini, squash, green chilies, mushrooms, fajita seasoning, garlic salt, and pepper. Stir over medium heat just until vegetables are tender. **Do not overcook!** Stir in cheese just before serving. Spoon mixture on tortillas and roll. Garnish with salsa if desired.

Recipe makes 6 servings.

Each serving provides:

158	Calories	3.5 g	Dietary fiber
2.4 g	Fat	524 mg	Sodium
7.5 g	Protein	2 mg	Cholesterol
27.9 g	Carbohydrates		

Salmon Cakes

Salmon Cakes
1 can (6⅛ ounces) salmon, drained
2 tablespoons chopped onion
2 egg whites, slightly beaten
2 teaspoons lemon juice
½ teaspoon seasoned salt (optional)
Black pepper to taste
¼ cup fat-free cracker crumbs
½ cup cornmeal

White Sauce
½ cup evaporated skim milk
½ cup skim milk
2 teaspoons Molly McButter
1 teaspoon dill weed
1 tablespoon lemon juice
Salt and black pepper to taste
2 tablespoons all-purpose flour

In medium bowl, combine salmon, onion, egg whites, lemon juice, seasoned salt, pepper, and cracker crumbs and mix thoroughly. Form into patties and roll in cornmeal. Cook in skillet sprayed with nonstick cooking spray over medium to low heat 5–6 minutes on each side or until brown.

In small saucepan, combine all sauce ingredients except flour. Use a whisk to blend in flour and stir over medium heat until slightly thickened. Pour over salmon cakes and serve.

Recipe makes 3 servings.

Each serving provides:

291	Calories	1.8 g	Dietary fiber
5.2 g	Fat	533 mg	Sodium
19.8 g	Protein	34 mg	Cholesterol
39.7 g	Carbohydrates		

Cream Cheese Chicken Salad Pockets

½ pound boneless, skinless chicken breasts,
    cut into small pieces
Garlic powder
Black pepper
2 tablespoons fat-free Italian salad dressing
1 large tomato, chopped into small chunks
1 medium cucumber, chopped into small chunks
5 green onions, thinly sliced
½ cup (4 ounces) Kraft fat-free cream cheese
1 clove garlic, pressed
½ teaspoon seasoned salt (optional)
3 pita breads (cut in half to make 6 pockets)

Season chicken pieces lightly with garlic powder and pepper. Brown in skillet sprayed with nonstick cooking spray. Add Italian dressing and simmer until chicken is done. Set aside to cool.

In large bowl, combine vegetables, cream cheese, garlic, and seasoned salt and mix thoroughly. Add cooked chicken and mix. Chill and serve in pita pockets.

Recipe makes 6 servings.

Each serving provides:

129	Calories	1.3 g	Dietary fiber
0.9 g	Fat	238 mg	Sodium
14.1 g	Protein	25 mg	Cholesterol
15.8 g	Carbohydrates		

White Chili

—⁂—

1 package (16 ounces) dry white beans
2 cans (14 ounces each) fat-free chicken broth
1½ cups water
2 boneless, skinless chicken breasts, cut into small pieces
    (8 ounces total)
1 medium onion, chopped
1 stalk celery, chopped
1 can (4 ounces) chopped green chilies
1 clove garlic, pressed
½ teaspoon chili powder
Salt and pepper to taste
½ cup fat-free sour cream

Rinse beans and cover with water. Bring to boil; turn off heat and let stand 1 hour and drain. Add chicken broth and 1½ cups water and simmer.

In skillet sprayed with nonstick cooking spray, brown chicken pieces, onion, and celery. Add to beans along with all remaining ingredients except sour cream. Simmer 2–3 hours or until beans are done. Add sour cream just before serving.

Recipe makes 6 servings.

Each serving provides:

341	Calories	12.3 g	Dietary fiber
2.5 g	Fat	719 mg	Sodium
30 g	Protein	22 mg	Cholesterol
51.7 g	Carbohydrates		

Pasta–Vegetable Casserole

———❦———

1 can (10¾ ounces) Campbell's 98 percent fat-free
    cream of mushroom soup
1 can (10¾ ounces) Campbell's 99 percent fat-free
    tomato soup
1 can (5 ounces) evaporated skim milk
1 cup grated fat-free American cheese
Dash of Tabasco sauce
½ teaspoon seasoned salt (optional)
Salt to taste
½ teaspoon black pepper
1 yellow squash, diced
1 medium onion, chopped
1 tablespoon chopped green pepper
2 cups (½ pound) fresh mushrooms, sliced
6 cups cooked pasta

Preheat oven to 350 degrees F

In large bowl, combine cream of mushroom soup, tomato soup, and evaporated milk and mix with electric mixer until smooth. By hand, fold in cheese, Tabasco sauce, seasoned salt, salt, and pepper. Add squash, onion, green pepper, mushrooms, and pasta and stir. Bake in large casserole sprayed with nonstick cooking spray for 45–50 minutes.

Recipe makes 8 servings.

Each serving provides:

254	Calories	3.1 g	Dietary fiber
2.3 g	Fat	436 mg	Sodium
12.7 g	Protein	5 mg	Cholesterol
45.5 g	Carbohydrates		

Chilled Cream Cheese Veggie Pizza

⎯⎯⎯✥⎯⎯⎯

⅓ cup (3 ounces) Kraft fat-free cream cheese
¼ teaspoon garlic powder
1 teaspoon dry onion flakes
¼ teaspoon seasoned salt
1 small Boboli pizza crust (single serving size)
2 tablespoons canned mushrooms, drained
1 tablespoon chopped green pepper
1 green onion, chopped
5 slices cucumber
Garlic salt to taste
Seasoned salt to taste

In small bowl, combine cream cheese, garlic powder, onion flakes, and seasoned salt. Mix thoroughly and spread on pizza crust. Layer with vegetables and sprinkle with garlic salt and seasoned salt. Eat immediately or chill before serving; either way is delicious.

Recipe makes 1 serving.

Each serving provides:

397	Calories	3.3 g	Dietary fiber
7.1 g	Fat	1508 mg	Sodium
26 g	Protein	19 mg	Cholesterol
60 g	Carbohydrates		

Blackened Orange Shrimp

—⚜—

¾ cup orange juice concentrate
Grated peel from 1 orange
2 teaspoons lite soy sauce
12 large shrimp
Blackened or Cajun spices to taste
Garlic salt to taste

Preheat oven to 350 degrees F

In small bowl, combine orange juice concentrate, grated
orange peel, and soy sauce.

Season both sides of shrimp heavily with blackened
spices and lightly with garlic salt. Brown on each side in
large skillet sprayed with nonstick cooking spray.
Transfer to square or round baking dish sprayed with
nonstick cooking spray and pour orange juice mixture on
top. Bake for 30–35 minutes.

Recipe makes 4 servings.

Each serving provides:

122	Calories	0.6 g	Dietary fiber
0.5 g	Fat	184 mg	Sodium
8.9 g	Protein	70 mg	Cholesterol
20.6 g	Carbohydrates		

Chicken Marsala with Angel Hair Pasta

8 ounces dry angel hair pasta
4 boneless, skinless chicken breasts
Garlic powder
Black pepper

Sauce:
¼ cup marsala cooking wine (available at most
    grocery stores)
1½ cups fat-free chicken broth
1½ tablespoons Molly McButter
1 teaspoon dry onion flakes
1 clove garlic, pressed
¼ cup evaporated skim milk
1 cup (¼ pound) fresh mushrooms, sliced
Black pepper to taste
1 tablespoon cornstarch
¼ cup cold water

Prepare angel hair pasta according to package directions, using no oil.

    Season chicken breasts lightly with garlic powder and pepper. Cook in skillet sprayed with nonstick cooking spray until golden brown and done. Remove from skillet and set aside.

Pour cooking wine into skillet and stir over low heat 1 minute. Add chicken broth, Molly McButter, onion flakes, and garlic and stir 1 minute. Add evaporated milk and mushrooms and simmer and stir until mushrooms are done, 2–3 minutes. Add pepper.

In small bowl, mix cornstarch and cold water until smooth. Add to skillet and stir until sauce thickens. Remove from heat.

Place a mound of pasta on each plate. Place 1 chicken breast on each mound and pour equal parts of sauce over each. Serve and enjoy.

Recipe makes 4 servings.

Each serving provides:

396	Calories	2.8 g	Dietary fiber
2.6 g	Fat	602 mg	Sodium
37.2 g	Protein	69 mg	Cholesterol
52.5 g	Carbohydrates		

Pizza Burger

1 pound ground turkey breast or chicken breast
½ bell pepper, sliced
1 medium onion, sliced
2 cups (½ pound) fresh mushrooms, sliced
Garlic salt to taste
Black pepper to taste
6 lite hamburger buns
½ cup lowfat pizza sauce
1 cup shredded fat-free mozzarella cheese

Form meat into 6 patties and brown and cook in skillet sprayed with nonstick cooking spray; season to taste and set aside.

In large skillet sprayed with nonstick cooking spray, brown and sauté bell pepper, onion, and mushrooms. Sprinkle with garlic salt and pepper.

Assemble each burger with bun, meat patty, pizza sauce, cheese, and vegetable mixture. Place, open-faced, on baking sheet and place under broiler just long enough for sauce to heat and cheese to melt. Remove and place top bun on.

Recipe makes 6 servings.

Each serving provides:

293	Calories	1.9 g	Dietary fiber
3.3 g	Fat	569 mg	Sodium
30.2 g	Protein	49 mg	Cholesterol
35.1 g	Carbohydrates		

Spicy Oven Chicken

———❧———

½ cup skim milk
1 teaspoon lite soy sauce
½ teaspoon Tabasco sauce
½ teaspoon Worcestershire sauce
1 tablespoon spicy hot mustard
1 clove garlic, pressed
¾ cup all-purpose flour
Salt to taste
¼ teaspoon black pepper
1 tablespoon dry taco seasoning
4 boneless, skinless chicken breasts

Preheat oven to 350 degrees F

In small bowl, mix milk, soy sauce, Tabasco sauce,
Worcestershire sauce, mustard, and garlic. In another
bowl, mix flour, salt, pepper, and taco seasoning.

Dip chicken breasts in milk mixture, then in flour mixture and bake on baking sheet sprayed with nonstick cooking spray for 35–40 minutes. Spray top of chicken with small amount of butter-flavored nonstick spray before serving.

Recipe makes 4 servings.

Each serving provides:

237	Calories	1 g	Dietary fiber
2 g	Fat	364 mg	Sodium
31.3 g	Protein	69 mg	Cholesterol
21.3 g	Carbohydrates		

Spaghetti Casserole

1 pound ground turkey breast or chicken breast
1 medium onion, chopped
1½ cups (6 ounces) fresh mushrooms, sliced and sautéed
1 clove garlic, pressed
1 can (16 ounces) chopped tomatoes
1 can (8 ounces) tomato sauce
1 package (1⅓ ounces) dry spaghetti sauce mix
1 package(8 ounces) spaghetti, broken, cooked,
    and drained
½ cup shredded fat-free mozzarella cheese
½ cup fat-free Parmesan cheese

Preheat oven to 375 degrees F

Brown meat and onion in large skillet sprayed with non-stick cooking spray. Add mushrooms; simmer and stir 5 minutes. Add garlic, tomatoes, and tomato sauce and simmer 5 more minutes. Add spaghetti sauce mix and stir. Pour mixture over spaghetti and toss.

Pour half the mixture into large casserole sprayed with nonstick cooking spray. Sprinkle with mozzarella cheese and add remaining spaghetti mixture. Top with Parmesan and bake for 30–35 minutes.

Recipe makes 8 servings.

Each serving provides:

252	Calories	2.6 g	Dietary fiber
1.7 g	Fat	646 mg	Sodium
22.3 g	Protein	38 mg	Cholesterol
35.2 g	Carbohydrates		

Egg Foo Yung

Patties
½ cup shredded carrots
2 green onions, chopped
2 cups bean sprouts
1 clove garlic, pressed
1½ cups fat-free liquid egg product
Salt and black pepper to taste

Sauce
1 cup canned vegetable broth
2 teaspoons sugar
2 teaspoons white vinegar
1 tablespoon lite soy sauce
2 tablespoons water
1 tablespoon cornstarch

Add carrots to large skillet sprayed with nonstick cooking spray and stir over medium heat 2–3 minutes. Add onions, bean sprouts, and garlic and remove from heat.

In large bowl, beat egg product and add salt and pepper. Add vegetable mixture and stir.

Spray skillet again with nonstick cooking spray. Using about ⅓ cup at a time, place mixture in skillet to form patties. Cook until egg is set, then turn and cook on other side. Repeat until all mixture is used.

In small saucepan, heat broth, sugar, vinegar, and soy sauce. In small cup or bowl, stir together water and cornstarch. Add to saucepan and stir until thickened. Pour over Egg Foo Yung patties.

Recipe makes 6 servings.

Each serving provides:

65	Calories	1.1 g	Dietary fiber
0.3 g	Fat	374 mg	Sodium
7.5 g	Protein	0 mg	Cholesterol
8.7 g	Carbohydrates		

Chicken Gumbo Burgers

1 pound ground chicken breast or turkey breast
½ medium onion, chopped
1 can (15 ounces) Healthy Choice chicken with
    rice soup
1 tablespoon ketchup
1 tablespoon mustard

In skillet sprayed with nonstick cooking spray, brown
meat with onion. Add remaining ingredients and
simmer over low heat 20–30 minutes. Serve on lite
hamburger buns.

Recipe makes 6 servings.

Each serving provides:

124	Calories	0.9 g	Dietary fiber
1.7 g	Fat	244 mg	Sodium
19.9 g	Protein	47 mg	Cholesterol
6 g	Carbohydrates		

Sweet Onion Sandwich

———✦———

Nonfat butter-flavored nonstick cooking spray
2 medium sweet Vidalia onions, sliced
Garlic salt to taste
Black pepper to taste
4 slices sourdough bread
2 slices fat-free Swiss cheese

Preheat oven to 375 degrees F

In large skillet sprayed with nonstick cooking spray,
brown and sauté onions over medium heat, adding garlic
salt and pepper while cooking.

Spray 1 side of bread slices with nonstick cooking
spray and toast.

Place thick pile of cooked onions on 2 slices toast
and top each with 1 slice cheese. Warm in oven long
enough to melt cheese. Top with bread slice and
serve warm.

Recipe makes 2 servings.

Each serving provides:

248	Calories	4.2 g	Dietary fiber
0.9 g	Fat	430 mg	Sodium
12.1 g	Protein	2 mg	Cholesterol
46.3 g	Carbohydrates		

Pasta Salad with Honey Mustard Chicken

Sauce
¼ cup honey
¼ cup spicy mustard
1 teaspoon lemon juice
½ teaspoon grated lemon peel
1 teaspoon lite soy sauce
½ teaspoon garlic salt

Salad
4 boneless, skinless chicken breasts, cut into small pieces
Salt and black pepper to taste
5 cups cooked pasta shells
1 can (14 ounces) artichoke hearts in water, drained
    and quartered
1 bottle (8 ounces) fat-free Italian dressing or fat-free
    honey-Dijon dressing

In small bowl, combine all sauce ingredients.

Brown chicken pieces in large skillet sprayed with nonstick cooking spray. While browning, add salt and pepper. Add sauce to browned chicken and simmer over low heat until most of sauce has been absorbed. Set aside to cool.

Combine pasta, artichoke hearts, and cooled chicken and toss. Add ½ bottle of dressing and chill. Add remaining dressing just before serving.

Recipe makes 6 servings.

Each serving provides:

338	Calories	2.4 g	Dietary fiber
2.3 g	Fat	575 mg	Sodium
25.7 g	Protein	46 mg	Cholesterol
53 g	Carbohydrates		

Ham, Cheese, and Asparagus Rolls

¼ cup (2 ounces) Kraft fat-free cream cheese
½ teaspoon garlic salt
⅛ teaspoon black pepper
¼ cup fat-free Parmesan cheese
1½ teaspoons horseradish
4 egg roll wrappers
4 slices Healthy Choice sliced ham
8 asparagus spears, cooked
4 slices Kraft fat-free Swiss cheese
1 egg white, slightly beaten
½ teaspoon sesame seeds

Preheat oven to 375 degrees F

In small bowl, combine cream cheese, garlic salt, pepper, Parmesan, and horseradish. Mix thoroughly.

Place 1 egg roll wrapper at a time on dinner plate and place 1 ham slice in center. Spread about 2 teaspoons cream cheese mixture in center of ham; then place 2 spears asparagus across ham and top with 1 slice cheese. Starting at corner, roll wrapper on the diagonal. On first roll, fold each end in toward center and continue rolling. Brush a little egg white on ends on last roll to hold it together.

Place finished rolls on baking sheet sprayed with nonstick cooking spray. Sprinkle sesame seeds on tops and bake for 15–20 minutes or until golden brown.

Recipe makes 4 servings.

Each serving provides:

185	Calories	1.5 g	Dietary fiber
0.5 g	Fat	656 mg	Sodium
15.6 g	Protein	10 mg	Cholesterol
29.4 g	Carbohydrates		

Bacon with Brown Sugar

4 slices turkey bacon
¼ cup brown sugar

In nonstick skillet, brown turkey bacon on one side.
Turn; sprinkle with brown sugar and continue cooking.
Turn once more and cook slightly at medium heat. If
heat is too high, sugar will scorch. Remove and serve.
Do not put on paper towels to cool.

Recipe makes 2 servings.

Each serving provides:

158	Calories	0 g	Dietary fiber
2.9 g	Fat	392 mg	Sodium
4.8 g	Protein	20 mg	Cholesterol
28.6 g	Carbohydrates		

Shrimp Fettuccini with Creamy Cheese Sauce

¾ cup evaporated skim milk
¾ cup skim milk
¾ cup (6 ounces) Kraft fat-free cream cheese
½ cup fat-free Parmesan cheese
1 tablespoon Molly McButter
1 pound cooked shrimp
Salt and black pepper to taste
4 cups fettuccini, cooked and drained

Preheat oven to 350 degrees F

In food processor, combine evaporated milk, skim milk, cream cheese, Parmesan, and Molly McButter. Transfer to saucepan and stir over medium heat until smooth and warm. Add shrimp, salt, and pepper; stir and simmer 1–2 minutes. Serve over fettuccini.

Recipe makes 4 servings.

Each serving provides:

445	Calories	2.2 g	Dietary fiber
2.3 g	Fat	803 mg	Sodium
43.7 g	Protein	238 mg	Cholesterol
57.2 g	Carbohydrates		

Tostadas

6 small corn tortillas
Nonfat butter-flavored nonstick cooking spray
Garlic salt
1 can (16 ounces) fat-free refried beans
½ cup fat-free sour cream
1 medium onion, chopped
1 cup grated fat-free Cheddar cheese
1 large tomato, chopped
2–3 cups chopped lettuce

Preheat oven to 375 degrees F

Place tortillas on cookie sheet sprayed with nonstick cooking spray. Lightly spray tops of tortillas and sprinkle with garlic salt. Place another cookie sheet over top of tortillas so they will bake flat and not curl. Bake for 10–12 minutes. Remove and cool slightly.

Spread each tortilla with refried beans and sour cream and sprinkle tops with onion, cheese, tomato, and lettuce.

Recipe makes 6 servings.

Each serving provides:

208	Calories	7.1 g	Dietary fiber
1 g	Fat	586 mg	Sodium
14.3 g	Protein	3 mg	Cholesterol
38.8 g	Carbohydrates		

Shrimp Rockefeller

1 tablespoon lemon juice
1 tablespoon all-purpose flour
1 small onion, chopped
½ cup cooked spinach, chopped
1 tablespoon parsley
2 teaspoons Molly McButter
¼ cup fat-free liquid egg product
Salt and black pepper to taste
2 dozen medium shrimp, cooked and peeled
½ cup seasoned bread crumbs (look for lowest fat)

Preheat oven to 350 degrees F

In small bowl, gradually add lemon juice to flour to make thin paste. Stir until smooth. Add onion, spinach, parsley, Molly McButter, egg product, salt, and pepper.

Spray medium casserole with nonstick cooking spray and line bottom with shrimp. Pour spinach mixture over top and sprinkle with bread crumbs. Bake for 15–20 minutes.

Recipe makes 6 servings.

Each serving provides:

96	Calories	1 g	Dietary fiber
0.9 g	Fat	238 mg	Sodium
11.3 g	Protein	78 mg	Cholesterol
10.1 g	Carbohydrates		

Oven Lemon-Pepper Chicken

———— ✣ ————

¾ cup fat-free mayonnaise
1 clove garlic, pressed
1 tablespoon fresh lemon juice
Grated peel from 1 lemon
4 boneless, skinless chicken breasts
1½ cups crushed cornflakes
Black pepper to taste

Preheat oven to 350 degrees F

Mix together mayonnaise, garlic, lemon juice, and lemon peel. Dip and coat chicken breasts in mixture and roll in crushed cornflakes. Place on baking sheet sprayed with nonstick cooking spray and sprinkle with pepper. Bake for 25–30 minutes.

Recipe makes 4 servings.

Each serving provides:

209	Calories	0.4 g	Dietary fiber
1.5 g	Fat	772 mg	Sodium
28.2 g	Protein	68 mg	Cholesterol
19.7 g	Carbohydrates		

Blackened Chicken Pasta

---

2 boneless, skinless chicken breasts, cut into
    bite-size pieces
½ cup fat-free Italian dressing
1 clove garlic, pressed
Blackened or Cajun spices
4 cups cooked pasta
1 can (14 ounces) water-packed artichoke hearts,
    drained

Marinate chicken pieces in combined Italian dressing
and garlic about 1 hour; discard marinade.

    Season chicken pieces heavily with blackened spices
and brown in skillet sprayed with nonstick cooking
spray over low heat until done. Cool.

    Combine chicken, pasta, and artichoke hearts.
Serve with your favorite dressing.

Recipe makes 4 servings.

Each serving provides:

299	Calories	3 g	Dietary fiber
1.8 g	Fat	281 mg	Sodium
22 g	Protein	34 mg	Cholesterol
48 g	Carbohydrates		

Rockefeller Casserole

2 slices turkey bacon
1 medium onion, chopped
1 box (10 ounces) frozen spinach, thawed and drained
3 medium yellow crookneck squash, diced
4 cups Kellogg's stuffing mix croutons
½ cup fat-free liquid egg product
1 can (14 ounces) fat-free chicken broth
Salt and black pepper to taste

Preheat oven to 325 degrees F

Brown and cook turkey bacon in nonstick skillet. Cool and crumble. Add onion to skillet and brown over medium heat.

Combine all ingredients and mix. Bake in large casserole sprayed with nonstick cooking spray for 45 minutes.

Recipe makes 8 servings.

Each serving provides:

115	Calories	3.2 g	Dietary fiber
0.7 g	Fat	550 mg	Sodium
7.5 g	Protein	3 mg	Cholesterol
21.1 g	Carbohydrates		

Chicken with Lemon Cream Sauce

4 boneless, skinless chicken breasts
Garlic salt to taste
Black pepper to taste
1 cup fat-free chicken broth
1½ tablespoons fresh lemon juice
1 teaspoon grated lemon peel
¼ cup fat-free Parmesan cheese
⅓ cup fat-free sour cream
1 tablespoon all-purpose flour

Season chicken breasts with garlic salt and pepper.
In skillet sprayed with nonstick cooking spray, brown
and cook over medium heat until done, 4–5 minutes
each side.

In medium saucepan, combine chicken broth, lemon juice, lemon peel, Parmesan, and sour cream. Use whisk to stir until smooth. Add 2–3 tablespoons mixture to flour to make a thin paste. Add paste back into sauce and stir over medium heat until thickened. Pour over chicken breasts and serve.

Recipe makes 4 servings.

Each serving provides:

175	Calories	0.1 g	Dietary fiber
1.5 g	Fat	406 mg	Sodium
30.4 g	Protein	71 mg	Cholesterol
7.6 g	Carbohydrates		

Pasta Primavera

Pasta
1 cup fresh broccoli pieces
1 cup sliced carrots
1 cup sliced zucchini
1½ cups (6 ounces) fresh mushrooms, sliced
1 large tomato, chopped
1 cup fresh snow peas
4 cups linguine noodles, cooked (8 ounces uncooked)

Sauce
½ cup evaporated skim milk
1 cup skim milk
¾ cup fat-free chicken broth
½ cup fat-free sour cream
½ cup fat-free Parmesan cheese
3 cloves garlic, pressed
2 teaspoons Molly McButter
Salt and black pepper to taste
2 tablespoons all-purpose flour

Steam or sauté vegetables and set aside while preparing sauce.

Combine all sauce ingredients except flour. Combine small amount of mixture with flour to make a thin paste. Pour back into sauce and stir over medium heat until slightly thickened.

Pour vegetables over noodles and pour sauce over top. Toss and serve warm.

Recipe makes 8 servings.

Each serving provides:

193	Calories	2.9 g	Dietary fiber
0.8 g	Fat	265 mg	Sodium
9.8 g	Protein	4 mg	Cholesterol
36 g	Carbohydrates		

Breakfast Pizzas

½ package (6 ounces) turkey sausage
4 slices turkey bacon
1 can (10¾ ounces) Campbell's 98 percent fat-free
    cream of mushroom soup
¼ cup skim milk
1 carton (8 ounces) fat-free liquid egg product
2 tablespoons Kraft fat-free cream cheese
½ green or red pepper, chopped
¼ cup chopped onion
Salt and black pepper to taste
1 can (7½ ounces) refrigerated no-fat biscuits
1 cup shredded fat-free Cheddar cheese

Preheat oven to 375 degrees F

Cook turkey sausage in skillet; drain and set aside. Cook
turkey bacon in skillet or microwave; crumble and set
aside. Combine mushroom soup with milk and set aside.
In skillet sprayed with nonstick cooking spray, sauté
pepper and onion until tender and set aside.

In skillet sprayed with nonstick cooking spray, combine egg product and cream cheese and cook until not quite done. Remove from heat and add red or green pepper, onion, sausage, bacon, salt, and pepper.

Spray cookie sheet with nonstick cooking spray. Press each biscuit onto cookie sheet to make 4-inch circle. Place large spoonful of egg mixture on each and top with large spoonful of soup mixture. Sprinkle with shredded cheese. Bake for 10–12 minutes.

Recipe makes 8 servings.

Each serving provides:

162	Calories	0.2 g	Dietary fiber
3.8 g	Fat	823 mg	Sodium
13.3 g	Protein	18 mg	Cholesterol
18.3 g	Carbohydrates		

Creamy Chicken and Artichoke Hearts over Noodles

4 boneless, skinless chicken breasts
2 cans (14 ounces each) fat-free chicken broth
Celery, carrot, and onion, chopped (seasoning for broth)
1 can (12 ounces) evaporated skim milk
¼ cup all-purpose flour
3 slices fat-free Cheddar cheese
3 slices fat-free Swiss cheese
½ teaspoon cayenne pepper
Salt to taste
1 can (4 ounces) button mushrooms, drained
1 can (14 ounces) artichoke hearts, drained
    and quartered
½ cup fat-free sour cream
1 clove garlic, pressed
½ package (12 ounces) No Yolk noodles, cooked
    and drained

Preheat oven to 350 degrees F

Simmer chicken breasts until tender in chicken broth seasoned with celery, carrot, and onion. Cut chicken into pieces and set aside. Reserve ½ cup chicken broth and discard celery, carrot, and onion.

In saucepan, combine evaporated milk, reserved ½ cup chicken broth, and flour. Whisk until smooth and cook over low heat, stirring constantly, until thickened.

Cut cheeses into small pieces and add to sauce, stirring until melted. Add chicken, seasonings, mushrooms, artichoke hearts, sour cream, and garlic. Bake for 20 minutes in casserole sprayed with nonstick cooking spray. Serve over noodles.

Recipe makes 4 servings.

Each serving provides:

505	Calories	2.4 g	Dietary fiber
4.3 g	Fat	876 mg	Sodium
57.6 g	Protein	83 mg	Cholesterol
56.4 g	Carbohydrates		

Santa Fe Pizza

Sauce
2 tablespoons fat-free chicken broth
1½ teaspoons Molly McButter
1 clove garlic, pressed
2 tablespoons finely chopped fresh sweet basil

Pizza
1 small Boboli pizza crust (single serving size)
1 small fresh green chili, sliced
2 tablespoons fat-free Parmesan cheese
3 ounces boneless, skinless chicken breasts, cooked and
    cut into strips (charcoal grilled if possible)
2 slices sweet Vidalia onion
¼ cup shredded fat-free mozzarella cheese

Preheat oven to 400 degrees F

Combine all sauce ingredients and brush onto pizza crust. Layer with green chili, Parmesan, chicken strips, onion, and mozzarella cheese. Place on baking sheet sprayed with nonstick cooking spray and cook for 12–15 minutes.

Recipe makes 2 servings.

Each serving provides:

257	Calories	1.7 g	Dietary fiber
4.1 g	Fat	704 mg	Sodium
22.7 g	Protein	32 mg	Cholesterol
32.5 g	Carbohydrates		

Hot Brown Sandwich

Sauce
1 small onion, chopped
3 tablespoons all-purpose flour
½ cup evaporated skim milk
1½ cups skim milk
¼ cup fat-free Parmesan cheese
¼ cup shredded fat-free Cheddar cheese
Salt and black or white pepper to taste

Topping
2 cups (½ pound) fresh sliced mushrooms
4 slices turkey bacon

Sandwich Base
8 slices lowfat bread, toasted
8 slices turkey breast

In large skillet sprayed with nonstick cooking spray, sauté onion until transparent. Add flour, evaporated milk, and skim milk and whisk until smooth. Cook over medium heat until sauce begins to thicken. Add cheeses and continue stirring over heat until well blended. Add salt and pepper and remove from heat.

In large skillet sprayed with nonstick cooking spray, sauté mushrooms until tender. Cook and crumble turkey bacon.

Prepare each sandwich in small oven-proof individual serving dishes. On each dish, place 1 slice of toast. Cover with 2 slices turkey breast; then spoon cheese sauce over each. Place under broiler until sauce begins to bubble. Cut remaining toast diagonally and place at each end of sandwich. Top with mushrooms and bacon and serve hot.

Recipe makes 4 sandwiches.

Each serving provides:

356	Calories	2.4 g	Dietary fiber
2.7 g	Fat	1108 mg	Sodium
28.8 g	Protein	31 mg	Cholesterol
52.3 g	Carbohydrates		

Vegetarian Enchiladas

1 carrot, sliced
½ cup fat-free chicken broth
1½ cups (6 ounces) fresh mushrooms, sliced
1 small zucchini, sliced
1 small yellow squash, sliced
1 medium onion, sliced
2 fresh green chilies, sliced
1 tablespoon chopped fresh cilantro
1 package (1¼ ounces) dry taco seasoning
½ teaspoon garlic salt
1 clove garlic, pressed
1 medium tomato, chopped
6 small fat-free flour tortillas

Topping
⅓ cup evaporated skim milk
½ cup shredded fat-free mozzarella cheese
2 green onions (including tops), chopped
½ teaspoon garlic salt

Preheat oven to 350 degrees F

Add carrot and small amount of chicken broth to large skillet sprayed with nonstick cooking spray. Simmer and stir. Add mushrooms and simmer 2–3 minutes. Add zucchini, yellow squash, onion, green chilies, cilantro, taco seasoning, garlic salt, and garlic. Pour in a little more chicken broth; simmer and stir until vegetables are partially done. Add tomato. **Do not overcook;** leave some crunch in the vegetables. Remove from heat and cool slightly.

Place about ½ cup mixture on each tortilla and roll; arrange in baking dish sprayed with nonstick cooking spray. Combine all topping ingredients and pour over enchiladas. Bake for 25–30 minutes. Garnish with salsa or fat-free sour cream if desired.

Recipe makes 6 servings.

Each serving provides:

175	Calories	4.6 g	Dietary fiber
4.8 g	Fat	1033 mg	Sodium
8 g	Protein	2 mg	Cholesterol
26.6 g	Carbohydrates		

Orange Marmalade Chicken

———❦———

1 pound boneless, skinless chicken breasts
$\frac{1}{2}$ teaspoon Molly McButter
1 jar (12 ounces) sweet orange marmalade
$\frac{1}{3}$ cup fat-free chicken broth
1 package (4.3 ounces) dry Lipton onion soup mix
4 cups rice, cooked

Preheat oven to 350 degrees F

Place chicken in 8-inch baking dish sprayed with non-stick cooking spray; sprinkle with Molly McButter.

In medium bowl, combine orange marmalade, chicken broth, and onion soup mix. Pour over chicken and bake for 45 minutes. Serve over rice.

Recipe makes 4 servings.

Each serving provides:

803	Calories	1.8 g	Dietary fiber
3.8 g	Fat	2897 mg	Sodium
35.3 g	Protein	67 mg	Cholesterol
145.8 g	Carbohydrates		

Pies, Pastries, and Desserts

Orange Poppy Seed Cake
Pumpkin Cheesecake
Chocolate Swirl Pie
Creamy Peanut Butter Dessert
Homemade Strawberry Ice Cream
Maurice's Creamy Raspberry Jell-O
Alice's Lemon Bars
Lemon Sour Cream Cake
Zesty Orange Cake
Strawberry Dream
Old-Fashioned Tapioca Pudding
Lemon Cheesecake
Strawberries and Cream Dessert
Cranberry Supreme
Apple Cinnamon Cobbler
Layered Chocolate Dream Dessert
Lemon Chess Pie
Pineapple Cream Pie
Peach Cobbler
Custard Pie
Chocolate Chip Pie

Chocolate Cheesecake
Cherry Sour Cream Cake
Old-Fashioned Blackberry Cobbler
Banana Cream Pudding
Noodle Pudding
Pecanless Pecan Pie
Strawberry Cream Cheese Pie
Caramel Apple Cake
Chocolate-Cherry Sour Cream Cake
Fancy Rice Pudding Dessert

Orange Poppy Seed Cake

1 package lowfat white cake mix
2 tablespoons poppy seeds
¾ cup fat-free liquid egg product
1 cup fat-free sour cream
1 can (6 ounces) frozen orange juice concentrate
⅓ cup water
2 teaspoons almond extract
½ teaspoon cinnamon
2 tablespoons sugar

Preheat oven to 350 degrees F

In large bowl, combine all ingredients except cinnamon and sugar and beat with electric mixer 2 minutes.

Spray Bundt pan with nonstick cooking spray. Combine sugar and cinnamon and sprinkle evenly over inside of pan. Pour in cake batter and bake for 45 minutes.

Recipe makes 12 servings.

Each serving provides:

144	Calories	0.6 g	Dietary fiber
2.1 g	Fat	111 mg	Sodium
4.2 g	Protein	0 mg	Cholesterol
27 g	Carbohydrates		

Pumpkin Cheesecake

Crust
8 graham cracker squares
2 tablespoons sugar

Filling
1 can (16 ounces) pumpkin
2 cups (16 ounces) fat-free cream cheese
1 cup fat-free sour cream
4 egg whites
2 cups brown sugar
1½ teaspoons pumpkin pie spice
¼ teaspoon salt
1 teaspoon vanilla extract

Preheat oven to 300 degrees F

In food processor, grind graham crackers; add sugar
and process lightly. Sprinkle mixture evenly over bottom
of large pie plate sprayed with nonstick cooking spray.
Set aside.

In food processor, combine all filling ingredients and process until well blended. Very carefully pour over crust, trying not to disturb crumbs. Bake for 55–60 minutes.

Recipe makes 8 servings.

Each serving provides:

362	Calories	2.1 g	Dietary fiber
0.7 g	Fat	468 mg	Sodium
12.9 g	Protein	9 mg	Cholesterol
76.7 g	Carbohydrates		

Chocolate Swirl Pie

—◦❦◦—

1 9-inch regular frozen Pet Ritz pie crust
1½ cups skim milk
1 package (3.4 ounces) chocolate cook and serve
    pudding
1 tub (8 ounces) fat-free cream cheese
1 teaspoon vanilla
¼ cup sugar
1 cup fat-free Cool Whip

Preheat oven to 425 degrees F

Remove frozen pie crust from the foil pan and place in glass pie plate. Bake according to package instructions. Remove from oven and cool.

Add milk to chocolate pudding mix and cook over medium-high heat until it thickens. Set aside to cool, stirring occasionally.

In large bowl, mix cream cheese, vanilla, and sugar with electric mixer until smooth. Add pudding mixture to bowl and blend on low speed.

To swirl

Add Cool Whip and only stir through a few times so it will leave swirls in the pudding. Pour into baked and cooled pie crust. Chill for 1–2 hours and serve.

Recipe makes 8 servings.

Each serving provides:

206	Calories	0 g	Dietary fiber
4.1 g	Fat	322 mg	Sodium
6.6 g	Protein	8 mg	Cholesterol
33.8 g	Carbohydrates		

Creamy Peanut Butter Dessert

Bottom layer
3 tablespoons graham cracker crumbs
1/4 teaspoon Molly McButter
1 teaspoon sugar

Filling
1 package (3 ounces) vanilla cook and serve pudding
2 cups skim milk
1 tub (8 ounces) fat-free cream cheese
1 teaspoon vanilla
1/4 cup sugar
2 tablespoons smooth peanut butter

Topping
1 cup fat-free Cool Whip
1–2 teaspoons graham cracker crumbs for garnish

Spray 9 × 9 inch square baking dish with nonstick
cooking spray. In small bowl, stir together all ingredients
for bottom layer. Sprinkle evenly over bottom of dish
and set aside.

Cook pudding according to package directions using skim milk. Stir over heat until pudding thickens. Set aside to cool.

In a large bowl, combine cream cheese, vanilla, sugar, and peanut butter. Mix with electric mixer until smooth. Mix in pudding. Pour onto bottom layer of graham cracker crumbs.

Chill for about 1 hour. Spread Cool Whip over top and sprinkle with 1–2 teaspoons graham cracker crumbs.

Recipe makes 9 servings.

Each serving provides:

146	Calories	0.3 g	Dietary fiber
2.1 g	Fat	270 mg	Sodium
6.5 g	Protein	5 mg	Cholesterol
24.8 g	Carbohydrates		

Homemade Strawberry Ice Cream

½ cup fat-free sour cream
2⅓ cups sugar
1½ cups fat-free liquid egg product
2 packages (10 ounces each) frozen strawberries
    with sugar
3 cans (12 ounces each) evaporated skim milk
2 teaspoons vanilla
⅛ teaspoon salt
Enough skim milk to fill freezer container to fill line
    (about 1 quart)

In large bowl, combine sour cream, sugar, and egg
product and mix with electric mixer. Add remaining
ingredients except skim milk and mix well. Pour into
freezer container and add skim milk. Freeze according
to freezer directions.

Recipe makes 16 servings.

Each serving provides:

234	Calories	0.7 g	Dietary fiber
0.4 g	Fat	175 mg	Sodium
10.5 g	Protein	4 mg	Cholesterol
49.3 g	Carbohydrates		

Maurice's Creamy Raspberry Jell-O

1 package (3 ounces) raspberry Jell-O
1 cup hot water
¾ cup fat-free sour cream
1 package (10 ounces) frozen raspberries with sugar

Stir Jell-O into hot water until completely dissolved. Add sour cream and beat with electric mixer until smooth. Add frozen raspberries and blend in food processor. Pour into mold or bowl and chill until set.

Recipe makes 8 servings.

Each serving provides:

93	Calories	0.8 g	Dietary fiber
0.1 g	Fat	44 mg	Sodium
2.6 g	Protein	0 mg	Cholesterol
21.4 g	Carbohydrates		

Recipe Contributed by: Maurice Gershon

Alice's Lemon Bars

Cake
1 package lowfat white cake mix
1 box (3 ounces) lemon gelatin
¾ cup fat-free liquid egg product
⅔ cup lemon juice
⅔ cup water
Grated peel from 1 lemon

Glaze
1½ cups powdered sugar
Juice of 2 lemons

Preheat oven to 350 degrees F

Combine all cake ingredients and beat with electric mixer 2 minutes. Pour into 11 × 14 inch pan sprayed with nonstick cooking spray and bake for 25–30 minutes.

In small bowl, combine powdered sugar and lemon juice and stir with spoon until smooth. Pour over warm cake. Cool and cut into squares.

Recipe makes 12 servings.

Each serving provides:

172	Calories	0.4 g	Dietary fiber
1.7 g	Fat	115 mg	Sodium
3 g	Protein	0 mg	Cholesterol
37 g	Carbohydrates		

Lemon Sour Cream Cake

Cake
1 package lowfat white cake mix
¾ cup lemon juice
¾ cup water
1 cup fat-free sour cream
Grated peel from 1 lemon
1 box (3 ounces) lemon gelatin
3 egg whites
½ teaspoon lemon extract

Glaze
1 cup powdered sugar
2 tablespoons lemon juice

Preheat oven to 350 degrees F

In large bowl, combine all cake ingredients and mix with electric mixer. Place in 9 × 13 inch glass baking dish sprayed with nonstick cooking spray and bake for 40–45 minutes.

In small bowl, combine glaze ingredients and stir by hand until smooth. Pour over warm cake.

Recipe makes 12 servings.

Each serving provides:

165	Calories	0.4 g	Dietary fiber
1.7 g	Fat	116 mg	Sodium
3.6 g	Protein	0 mg	Cholesterol
34.1 g	Carbohydrates		

Zesty Orange Cake

Cake
1 package lowfat white cake mix
3 egg whites
1 cup orange juice
1/3 cup lemon juice
Grated peel from 1 orange
1 cup fat-free sour cream
1 teaspoon orange extract

Glaze
1 cup powdered sugar
1 1/2 tablespoons orange juice concentrate
1 tablespoon lemon juice
1 teaspoon grated orange peel

Preheat oven to 350 degrees F

In large bowl, combine all cake ingredients and mix with electric mixer until thoroughly blended. Bake in 9 × 13 inch cake pan sprayed with nonstick cooking spray (use glass baking dish if possible) for 40–45 minutes.

In small bowl, combine all glaze ingredients; stir by hand until smooth. Pour over warm cake.

Recipe makes 12 servings.

Each serving provides:

149	Calories	0.5 g	Dietary fiber
1.7 g	Fat	99 mg	Sodium
3.3 g	Protein	0 mg	Cholesterol
30.1 g	Carbohydrates		

Strawberry Dream

Topping
1 cup Kraft fat-free cream cheese
⅓ cup sugar
⅓ cup fat-free sour cream
1 teaspoon vanilla extract

Suggestions for Shortcake
Fat-free pound cake
Angel food cake
Lowfat biscuits (add a little sugar to lowfat biscuit mix)

2 packages (10 ounces each) frozen sliced strawberries
   with sugar

Combine all topping ingredients and stir until smooth.
   For each serving, place your choice of shortcake on serving dish. Add several spoonfuls of strawberries and top with a few spoonfuls of topping. Enjoy.

Recipe makes 6 large servings.

Each serving provides:

192	Calories	1.8 g	Dietary fiber
0.1 g	Fat	282 mg	Sodium
9.4 g	Protein	9 mg	Cholesterol
40.5 g	Carbohydrates		

Old-Fashioned Tapioca Pudding

2 cups evaporated skim milk
1 cup skim milk
½ cup sugar
3½ tablespoons minute tapioca
¼ cup fat-free liquid egg product
1 teaspoon Molly McButter
1 teaspoon vanilla extract

In medium saucepan, combine all ingredients except vanilla; stir and let stand 5 minutes.
Stir over medium heat until mixture comes to boil. Remove from heat and add vanilla. Let cool 15–20 minutes. Mixture will thicken as it cools. Serve warm or chilled.

Recipe makes 6 servings.

Each serving provides:

167	Calories	0 g	Dietary fiber
0.3 g	Fat	166 mg	Sodium
8.8 g	Protein	4 mg	Cholesterol
32.5 g	Carbohydrates		

Lemon Cheesecake

Crust
8 graham cracker squares, ground
2 tablespoons sugar
2 teaspoons Molly McButter

Filling
1 cup fat-free sour cream
3 cartons (8 ounces each) Kraft fat-free cream cheese*
5 egg whites
1 cup sugar
4 tablespoons fresh lemon juice (about 2 lemons)
Grated peel from 1 lemon
$\frac{1}{4}$ teaspoon salt
2 tablespoons all-purpose flour

Preheat oven to 350 degrees F

In small bowl, combine all crust ingredients and mix.
Sprinkle evenly over bottom and a little on sides of
10-inch pie plate sprayed with nonstick cooking spray;
set aside.

*This recipe will turn out entirely different with other brands of
fat-free cream cheese. Use only Kraft fat-free cream cheese for
this recipe.

In food processor, combine all filling ingredients and process until thoroughly blended. Very gently pour over crust. Bake for 20 minutes. Reduce temperature to 225 degrees and bake additional 1 hour and 10 minutes. Remove from oven and cool.

Pie must be refrigerated several hours or overnight before slicing and serving.

Recipe makes 8 servings.

Each serving provides:

247	Calories	0.3 g	Dietary fiber
0.5 g	Fat	628 mg	Sodium
16.9 g	Protein	14 mg	Cholesterol
44 g	Carbohydrates		

Strawberries and Cream Dessert

2 cups fresh sliced or chopped strawberries
⅓ cup sugar
⅓ cup fat-free sour cream
1 cup fat-free Cool Whip
½ teaspoon vanilla

Stir together strawberries and sugar and set aside for 10 minutes, stirring occasionally. Add remaining ingredients and stir. Chill and serve. Great over a lowfat shortcake, if desired.

Recipe makes 4 servings.

Each serving provides:

127	Calories	1.7 g	Dietary fiber
0.3 g	Fat	24 mg	Sodium
1.8 g	Protein	0 mg	Cholesterol
29.1 g	Carbohydrates		

Cranberry Supreme

½ cup cold water
1 package (3 ounces) cranberry Jell-O
1 tub (8 ounces) fat-free cream cheese
1 cup fat-free Cool Whip
2 tablespoons frozen orange juice concentrate
½ teaspoon grated orange peel
¼ cup sugar

Combine water with Jell-O and mix. Set aside. In large bowl, cream fat-free cream cheese with electric mixer until very smooth. Combine all other ingredients and whip with electric mixer. Whip Jell-O mixture into cream mixture and chill 1–2 hours.

Recipe makes 10 servings.

Each serving provides:

89	Calories	0.1 g	Dietary fiber
0 g	Fat	134 mg	Sodium
4 g	Protein	4 mg	Cholesterol
18.1 g	Carbohydrates		

Apple Cinnamon Cobbler

Filling
1 can (20 ounces) sliced apples
⅔ cup sugar
2 teaspoons Molly McButter
1 teaspoon ground cinnamon

Crust
1½ cups lowfat biscuit mix (I like Pioneer brand if you
    can find it in your area. It is very low in fat.)
1¼ cups canned evaporated skim or fat-free canned milk
¼ cup sugar

1 tablespoon sugar for sprinkling on top

Preheat oven to 350 degrees F

In medium bowl, combine apples, sugar, Molly
McButter, and cinnamon. Stir and set aside.
    In another bowl, combine biscuit mix and milk.
Stir until blended, then add sugar and stir. Mixture will
be thin.

Spray 9 × 13 inch baking dish with nonstick cooking spray. Pour in half the crust batter mixture. Spread apple mixture evenly over top of batter. Pour the remaining batter over top and sprinkle top lightly with 1 tablespoon sugar.

Bake for 30 minutes. Great served hot with fat-free ice cream.

Recipe makes 8 servings.

Each serving provides:

281	Calories	1.9 g	Dietary fiber
0.8 g	Fat	477 mg	Sodium
5.5 g	Protein	2 mg	Cholesterol
70 g	Carbohydrates		

Layered Chocolate Dream Dessert

Snackwell's Devils food cookies
1 package (3⅜ ounces) Snackwell's Instant
    Pistachio pudding
1 box (3¼ ounces) chocolate Jell-O cook and
    serve pudding
2 cups skim milk
1 cup fat-free Cool Whip

Chop cookies in food processor and then divide cookie
crumb mixture in half.

Spray 7 × 11 inch casserole dish with nonstick
cooking spray. Sprinkle half of cookie mixture over
bottom of dish.

Mix pistachio pudding according to package
directions, using skim milk, and pour in dish over
cookie crumbs.

Cook chocolate pudding according to package directions, using skim milk. Set aside to cool slightly when done. Stir a couple of times. Stir in enough Cool Whip to swirl it through chocolate. Do not mix. Pour into dish with other layers. Sprinkle remaining cookie crumbs over top. Chill at least 1–2 hours and serve.

Recipe makes 8 servings.

Each serving provides:

174	Calories	0.5 g	Dietary fiber
0.2 g	Fat	328 mg	Sodium
3.1 g	Protein	1 mg	Cholesterol
40.7 g	Carbohydrates		

Lemon Chess Pie

Crust
½ cup Pioneer Low-Fat Biscuit Mix*
1 tablespoon sugar
1 teaspoon Molly McButter

Filling
1½ cups evaporated skim milk
1 cup fat-free liquid egg product
2 teaspoons Molly McButter
½ cup plus 3 tablespoons sugar
Juice from 2 lemons
Grated peel from 1 lemon
1 teaspoon vanilla extract

Preheat oven to 300 degrees F

In small bowl, combine all crust ingredients and stir.
Sprinkle evenly over bottom of 9-inch pie plate sprayed
with nonstick cooking spray and set aside.

*If you can't find Pioneer Low-Fat Biscuit Mix in your area, use
a light biscuit mix; however, this substitution will add a few grams
of fat to each serving.

In food processor, combine all filling ingredients and process. Pour very gently over crust mixture, trying not to disturb crust. Bake for 55–60 minutes. Cool and serve.

Recipe makes 8 servings.

Each serving provides:

166	Calories	0.2 g	Dietary fiber
0.3 g	Fat	302 mg	Sodium
7.5 g	Protein	2 mg	Cholesterol
35.9 g	Carbohydrates		

Pineapple Cream Pie

Crust
½ cup Grape Nuts cereal
2½ tablespoons sugar
½ teaspoon Molly McButter

Filling
¾ cup fat-free liquid egg product
1¼ cups sugar
⅓ cup all-purpose flour
⅓ cup (3 ounces) Kraft fat-free cream cheese
1 tablespoon Molly McButter
1 teaspoon vanilla extract
1 can (15¼ ounces) crushed pineapple in its own juice
    (pour off juice but do not squeeze all the liquid out)

Preheat oven to 325 degrees F

Pour Grape Nuts over bottom of 9-inch pie plate
sprayed with nonstick cooking spray. Sprinkle sugar and
Molly McButter evenly over Grape Nuts and set aside.

In medium bowl and using electric mixer, cream together all ingredients for filling except pineapple until smooth. Fold in pineapple with spoon. Carefully pour over crust, trying not to disturb Grape Nuts. Bake for 50–55 minutes.

Recipe makes 8 servings.

Each serving provides:

233	Calories	1.3 g	Dietary fiber
0.3 g	Fat	213 mg	Sodium
5.3 g	Protein	2 mg	Cholesterol
53.6 g	Carbohydrates		

Peach Cobbler

Filling
4 cups frozen or fresh peaches
¾ cup sugar
1 teaspoon lemon juice
1 teaspoon Molly McButter

Crust
1½ cups Pioneer Low-Fat Biscuit Mix*
1¼ cups evaporated skim milk
2 tablespoons sugar

Preheat oven to 350 degrees F

Combine all filling ingredients. Stir gently until sugar starts to dissolve and set aside.

Combine biscuit mix and evaporated milk and stir until well blended. Mixture will be like thin batter. Add sugar and mix.

*If you can't find Pioneer Low-Fat Biscuit Mix in your area, use a light biscuit mix; however, this substitution will add a few grams of fat to each serving.

Pour half the batter into 9 × 13 inch baking dish sprayed with nonstick cooking spray. Spoon fruit mixture evenly over top. Pour remaining batter evenly over top of peaches. Sprinkle a spoonful of granulated sugar over top. Bake for 30 minutes. Serve hot or cold.

Recipe makes 8 servings.

Each serving provides:

260	Calories	2.2 g	Dietary fiber
0.5 g	Fat	453 mg	Sodium
5.9 g	Protein	2 mg	Cholesterol
65.1 g	Carbohydrates		

Custard Pie

Crust
½ cup Pioneer Low-Fat Biscuit Mix*
1 teaspoon Molly McButter
1 tablespoon sugar

Filling
1 cup fat-free liquid egg product
½ cup plus 1 tablespoon sugar
1 cup evaporated skim milk
1 cup skim milk
2 teaspoons Molly McButter
1 teaspoon vanilla extract
1/4 teaspoon nutmeg

Preheat oven to 300 degrees F

In small bowl, combine all ingredients for crust. Sprinkle over bottom of large pie plate sprayed with nonstick cooking spray. Smooth with spoon to even out mixture over entire bottom. Set aside.

*If you can't find Pioneer Low-Fat Biscuit Mix in your area, use a light biscuit mix; however, this substitution will add a few grams of fat to each serving.

In food processor, combine all filling ingredients and mix well. Very carefully pour into pie plate, trying not to disturb crust. Bake for 45–55 minutes or until center is set.

Recipe makes 8 servings.

Each serving provides:

150	Calories	0.2 g	Dietary fiber
0.4 g	Fat	301 mg	Sodium
7.3 g	Protein	2 mg	Cholesterol
31.3 g	Carbohydrates		

Chocolate Chip Pie

Crust
1/2 cup Grape Nuts cereal
2 1/2 tablespoons sugar
1/2 teaspoon Molly McButter

Filling
1 cup fat-free liquid egg product
1 1/3 cups sugar
1/3 cup all-purpose flour
1 1/2 tablespoons Molly McButter
1 teaspoon vanilla extract
1/4 teaspoon almond extract
1/3 cup fat-free sour cream
1/3 cup regular-size semisweet chocolate chips
1/3 cup miniature semisweet chocolate chips

Preheat oven to 325 degrees F

Sprinkle Grape Nuts evenly over bottom of 9-inch pie plate sprayed with nonstick cooking spray. Sprinkle evenly with sugar and Molly McButter and set aside.

In medium bowl, using mixer, combine egg product, sugar, flour, Molly McButter, vanilla and almond extracts, and sour cream. Cream until smooth. Gently pour over Grape Nuts, trying not to disturb crust.

Using the regular-size chocolate chips, take a few at a time and drop each chip on top of filling, then fill in various places until all chips are used. These will gradually sink into filling. Bake for 50 minutes. Sprinkle miniature chips on top for garnish.

Recipe makes 8 servings.

Each serving provides:

277	Calories	1 g	Dietary fiber
5.5 g	Fat	212 mg	Sodium
5.6 g	Protein	0 mg	Cholesterol
54.9 g	Carbohydrates		

Chocolate Cheesecake

Crust
8 graham cracker squares, ground
2 tablespoons sugar
2 teaspoons Molly McButter

Filling
1 cup fat-free sour cream
3 cartons (8 ounces each) Kraft fat-free cream cheese*
5 egg whites
1 cup sugar
2 tablespoons Hershey's cocoa powder
2 teaspoons fresh lemon juice
$\frac{1}{4}$ teaspoon salt
2 tablespoons all-purpose flour

Preheat oven to 350 degrees F

In small bowl, mix all crust ingredients and sprinkle evenly over bottom of 10-inch pie plate sprayed with nonstick cooking spray. Set aside.

In food processor, combine all filling ingredients and process until thoroughly blended. Very gently pour over crust.

*This recipe will turn out entirely different with other brands of fat-free cream cheese. Use only Kraft fat-free cream cheese for this recipe.

Bake for 20 minutes; reduce temperature to 225 degrees and bake additional 1 hour and 10 minutes. Cool.

Pie must be refrigerated several hours or overnight before slicing and serving.

Recipe makes 8 servings.

Each serving provides:

251	Calories	0.3 g	Dietary fiber
0.7 g	Fat	628 mg	Sodium
17.1 g	Protein	14 mg	Cholesterol
44 g	Carbohydrates		

Cherry Sour Cream Cake

—❦—

1½ cups fat-free liquid egg product
½ cup fat-free cottage cheese
1 cup fat-free sour cream
1 tablespoon Molly McButter
1 teaspoon vanilla extract
1 cup sugar
2 cups Pioneer Low-Fat Biscuit Mix*
1 can (21 ounces) cherry pie filling

Preheat oven to 350 degrees F

Combine egg product, cottage cheese, sour cream, Molly McButter, vanilla, and sugar and beat with electric mixer 1–2 minutes.

*If you can't find Pioneer Low-Fat Biscuit Mix in your area, use a light biscuit mix; however, this substitution will add a few grams of fat to each serving.

Add biscuit mix and mix thoroughly. Fold in pie filling (do not mix). Pour mixture into 7 × 11 inch baking dish sprayed with nonstick cooking spray. Bake for 45 minutes.

Recipe makes 12 servings.

Each serving provides:

246	Calories	1.9 g	Dietary fiber
0.5 g	Fat	514 mg	Sodium
7.7 g	Protein	1 mg	Cholesterol
58.2 g	Carbohydrates		

Old-Fashioned Blackberry Cobbler

Filling
4 cups frozen blackberries, thawed
¾ cup sugar
1 teaspoon lemon juice
1 teaspoon Molly McButter

Crust
1½ cups Pioneer Low-Fat Biscuit Mix*
1¼ cups evaporated skim milk
¼ cup sugar

Preheat oven to 350 degrees F

Combine all filling ingredients. Stir gently until sugar
starts to dissolve and set aside.

Combine biscuit mix and milk and stir until
well blended. Mixture will be like thin batter. Add
sugar and mix.

*If you can't find Pioneer Low-Fat Biscuit Mix in your area, use
a light biscuit mix; however, this substitution will add a few grams
of fat to each serving.

Pour half the crust batter into 9 × 13 inch baking dish sprayed with nonstick cooking spray. Spoon berry mixture evenly over top. Pour remaining crust batter evenly over berries. Sprinkle a spoonful of granulated sugar over top. Bake for 30 minutes. Serve hot or cold.

Recipe makes 8 servings.

Each serving provides:

273	Calories	4.3 g	Dietary fiber
0.7 g	Fat	453 mg	Sodium
5.9 g	Protein	2 mg	Cholesterol
67.8 g	Carbohydrates		

Banana Cream Pudding

Bottom Layer
⅓ cup graham cracker crumbs
3 tablespoons sugar
2 teaspoons Molly McButter

Filling
1 package (3 ounces) cook and serve vanilla pudding
    and pie filling mix
1½ cups evaporated skim milk
½ cup skim milk
⅓ cup sugar
1 teaspoon Molly McButter
½ teaspoon vanilla extract
⅓ cup fat-free sour cream
3 large bananas, sliced

Topping
¼ cup graham cracker crumbs
2 tablespoons sugar

In small bowl, combine all ingredients for bottom layer and sprinkle evenly over bottom of 9-inch pie plate sprayed with nonstick cooking spray. Set aside.

In medium saucepan, combine pudding mix, evaporated milk, skim milk, sugar, and Molly McButter. Stir over medium heat until pudding comes to a boil. Remove from heat and add vanilla and sour cream. Mix with electric mixer until smooth and creamy. Add sliced bananas and spoon mixture into pie plate.

Combine topping ingredients and sprinkle over top. Chill to set.

Recipe makes 8 servings.

Each serving provides:

218	Calories	1.3 g	Dietary fiber
1 g	Fat	295 mg	Sodium
5.9 g	Protein	2 mg	Cholesterol
47.7 g	Carbohydrates		

Noodle Pudding

—✦—

1 package (8 ounces) No Yolk noodles
1 teaspoon Molly McButter
¾ cup sugar
1 cup fat-free cottage cheese
1 cup fat-free sour cream
1 cup (8 ounces) Kraft fat-free cream cheese, softened
½ teaspoon salt
2 teaspoons vanilla extract
1¼ cups fat-free liquid egg product
½ cup raisins (optional)
Cinnamon

Preheat oven to 350 degrees F

In large saucepan, cook noodles in boiling water until tender, 8–10 minutes. Drain and set aside.

In large bowl, beat together Molly McButter, sugar, cottage cheese, sour cream, cream cheese, salt, vanilla, egg product, and raisins. Stir in noodles.

Pour into 13 × 9 inch baking dish sprayed with nonstick cooking spray and sprinkle with cinnamon. Bake for 45–50 minutes. Let stand 5 minutes before cutting. Serve warm or cold.

Recipe makes 10 servings.

Each serving provides:

203	Calories	0.6 g	Dietary fiber
0.5 g	Fat	384 mg	Sodium
14 g	Protein	6 mg	Cholesterol
35.4 g	Carbohydrates		

Pecanless Pecan Pie

Crust
2 large fat-free flour tortillas
Buttermist or other butter-flavored nonstick
      cooking spray
½ teaspoon Molly McButter

Filling
¾ cup fat-free liquid egg product
½ cup light corn syrup
1 cup brown sugar
1 teaspoon all-purpose flour
1 tablespoon Molly McButter
1 teaspoon vanilla extract
⅓ cup Grape Nuts cereal

Preheat oven to 350 degrees F

Place 1 tortilla in 9-inch pie plate sprayed with nonstick cooking spray. Spray tortilla and sprinkle with Molly McButter. Place second tortilla on top and spray lightly with butter spray. Using another 9-inch pie plate, spray outside bottom and place on top of tortillas. This helps press and form pie crust. Bake crust with second pie plate on top for 7 minutes. Remove extra pie plate, cool crust slightly while preparing filling.

In large bowl, combine all ingredients except Grape Nuts and mix with electric mixer. Pour into partially baked crust. Sprinkle Grape Nuts over top of filling, and bake for 35 minutes. Do not cook longer than 35 minutes or filling might spill over sides while baking. Also, do not worry about how it looks while cooking because it will puff up high but will go back down as soon as it cools.

Recipe makes 8 servings.

Each serving provides:

238	Calories	1.7 g	Dietary fiber
0.5 g	Fat	198 mg	Sodium
3.9 g	Protein	0 mg	Cholesterol
55.7 g	Carbohydrates		

Strawberry
Cream Cheese Pie

Crust
2 large fat-free flour tortillas
Buttermist or other butter-flavored nonstick
    cooking spray
½ teaspoon Molly McButter

Filling
1 envelope Knox unflavored gelatin
½ cup hot water
1 package (16 ounces) frozen strawberries with sugar,
    thawed
1 cup Kraft fat-free cream cheese
⅓ cup sugar

Topping
½ envelope Knox unflavored gelatin
½ cup hot water
1½ cups fat-free sour cream
⅓ cup sugar
½ teaspoon vanilla extract

Preheat oven to 350 degrees F

Place 1 tortilla in deep 9½-inch pie plate sprayed with nonstick cooking spray. Spray tortilla lightly with butter spray and sprinkle with Molly McButter. Place second tortilla on top and spray lightly with butter spray. Spray outside bottom of another empty pie plate and set it inside and on top of tortillas for baking. Bake for 13 minutes. Remove and cool; remove extra pie plate. Cool thoroughly before adding filling.

Stir gelatin into hot water until dissolved. Combine with remaining ingredients in food processor. Pour into prepared crust.

Stir gelatin into hot water until dissolved. Combine with remaining ingredients and mix with electric mixer. Pour gently over filling. Chill several hours or overnight.

Recipe makes 10 servings.

Each serving provides:

179	Calories	1.9 g	Dietary fiber
0.4 g	Fat	210 mg	Sodium
8.8 g	Protein	5 mg	Cholesterol
36.4 g	Carbohydrates		

Caramel Apple Cake

Cake
2 large apples
2½ cups all-purpose flour
½ teaspoon baking soda
2 teaspoons baking powder
1½ teaspoons cinnamon
2 tablespoons Molly McButter
1½ cups sugar
½ cup fat-free liquid egg product
½ cup fat-free sour cream
3 pitted prunes
¾ cup evaporated skim milk
4 tablespoons fat-free caramel ice cream topping

Topping
¼ cup oatmeal
⅓ cup brown sugar
5–6 tablespoons fat-free caramel ice cream topping

Preheat oven to 350 degrees F

Peel and finely chop apples and set aside. Stir or sift together flour, baking soda, baking powder, cinnamon, and Molly McButter until thoroughly mixed.

In food processor, combine sugar, egg product, sour cream, prunes, and milk. Process until smooth. Pour mixture over apples and stir.

Using electric mixer, gradually add flour mixture to apple mixture and blend until all flour has been added. Pour into 9 × 13 inch glass baking dish that has been sprayed with nonstick cooking spray. Drizzle 4 tablespoons caramel topping over top.

In small bowl, combine oatmeal and brown sugar and sprinkle over top of cake batter. Drizzle 5–6 tablespoons caramel topping over top. Bake for 45–50 minutes. Test center with toothpick for doneness.

Recipe makes 12 servings.

Each serving provides:

377	Calories	1.6 g	Dietary fiber
0.5 g	Fat	344 mg	Sodium
6.5 g	Protein	1 mg	Cholesterol
88.8 g	Carbohydrates		

Chocolate-Cherry Sour Cream Cake

1½ cups all-purpose flour
⅓ cup dry cocoa
2 teaspoons Molly McButter
1 cup sugar
1 cup water
¼ cup light corn syrup
1 teaspoon vanilla extract
½ cup fat-free sour cream
½ teaspoon vinegar
½ teaspoon baking soda

Topping
¾ cup fat-free sour cream
⅓ cup sugar
1 can (21 ounces) cherry pie filling

Preheat oven to 350 degrees F

In large bowl, combine flour, cocoa, and Molly McButter; mix thoroughly.

Using electric mixer, combine sugar, water, corn syrup, vanilla, sour cream, vinegar, and baking soda. Mix until smooth. Add dry ingredients gradually. Pour in 9 × 13 baking dish sprayed with nonstick cooking spray.

In small bowl, combine sour cream and sugar and mix until smooth.

Drop pie filling by spoonfuls over top of cake batter and follow each spoonful with topping mixture. Bake for 45–50 minutes.

Recipe makes 12 servings.

Each serving provides:

155	Calories	0.4 g	Dietary fiber
0.5 g	Fat	97 mg	Sodium
2.8 g	Protein	0 mg	Cholesterol
35.7 g	Carbohydrates		

Fancy Rice Pudding Dessert

¾ cup (6 ounces) Kraft fat-free cream cheese
⅓ cup fat-free sour cream
½ cup sugar
½ teaspoon vanilla extract
2 cups cooked rice
1 jar (6 ounces) maraschino cherries, drained
1 can (8 ounces) crushed pineapple, drained
1½ cups miniature marshmallows

Cream together cream cheese, sour cream, sugar, and vanilla.

Combine remaining ingredients; pour over cream cheese mixture and stir. Chill and serve.

Recipe makes 8 servings.

Each serving provides:

212	Calories	0.9 g	Dietary fiber
0.2 g	Fat	113 mg	Sodium
5.5 g	Protein	3 mg	Cholesterol
47.5 g	Carbohydrates		

Index

Chicken
  and artichoke hearts over
    noodles, creamy, 266–267
  barbecue, and coleslaw
    sandwich, 178–179
  breasts
    with apricot-orange
      sauce, 174–175
    marinade, 127
    oven-fried, 166–167
    with wine sauce,
      162–163
  burgers
    gumbo, 246
    Mexican, 214
    pizza, 238–239
  creole gravy and rice with,
    204–205
  crispy buttermilk, 223
  with curry sauce, Erma's,
    156–157
  -fried chicken, with cream
    gravy, 164–165
  French onion and potato
    bake, 177
  goulash, Hungarian,
    150–151
  ground, spaghetti casserole,
    242–243
  gumbo, 210–211
  honey crunchy, 200–201
  honey Dijon
    crispy, 202–203
    oven-baked, 182
    sauce with, 148–149
  honey mustard, pasta salad
    with, 248–249
  jalapeño, 184
  kebabs, quick and easy,
    194–195
  lemon cream sauce with,
    260–261
  lemon-pepper, oven baked,
    257
  marsala with angel hair
    pasta, 236–237
  meatballs, oriental, 32–33
  meat loaf, onion mush
    room, 190
  Mexican layered dip, 19
  onion-mushroom, 201
  onion smothered, 157
  orange marmalade, 274
  pasta, blackened, 258
  pâté, 60
  pimiento, 180–181
    salad, 76
  rolls, sweet and sour, 6–7
  rotel, with sour cream,
    188–189

salads
  deluxe, 92
  pockets, with cream
    cheese, 228–229
  sweet and sour, 82–83
  taco, 84–85
Santa Fe pizza, 268–269
savory apricot, 183
spicy oven, 240–241
stuffed peppers, 213
tabasco, 176
Chile, *see* Green chile
Chili, 132–133
  dogs in a blanket,
    206–207
  white, 230–231
Chilled cream cheese veggie
  pizza, 234
Chocolate
  cheesecake, 314–315
  –cherry sour cream cake,
    328–329
  chip pie, 310–311
  layered dream dessert,
    300–301
  swirl pie, 280–281
Cinnamon
  apple cobbler, 298–299
  pull-aparts, 50–51
  roll-ups, 48–49
Clam
  dip, 53
  linguine, 185
Cobblers
  apple cinnamon, 298–299
  blackberry, old-fashioned,
    316–317
  peach, 306–307
Coleslaw
  and barbecue chicken
    sandwich, 178–179
  buttermilk, 77
Cookies, Alice's lemon bars,
  286–287
Corn, *see also* Hominy
  and black-eyed pea salad,
    106–107
  casserole, creamed, 130
  fancy, 69
  festive taco, 118
  quiche, 208
Corn bread
  dressing, holiday, 24–25
  onion bake, 42–43
  sweet, 63
Corn chip potato salad,
  100–101
Cranberry supreme, 297
Cream cheese
  chicken salad pockets,

228–229
garlic
  and cucumber spread, 27
  spread, 29
  and peaches gelatin
    salad, 95
  peanut butter dessert,
    282–283
  pesto with sun-dried
    tomatoes, 36–37
  pineapple pie, 304–305
  sandwiches on rye party
    bread, 11
  strawberry pie, 324–325
  veggie pizza, chilled, 234
  walnut-raisin, 18
Creamed corn casserole, 130
Cream gravy, chicken-fried
  chicken with, 164–165
Creamy chicken and
  artichoke hearts over
  noodles, 266–267
Creamy grapefruit-mandarin
  orange salad, 71
Creamy honey-mustard
  spread for sandwiches, 9
Creamy horseradish spread
  for sandwiches, 5
Creamy oven hash browns,
  102
Creamy peanut butter dessert,
  282–283
Creamy potatoes, 90–91
Creamy southwest soup, 89
Creole gravy chicken with
  rice, 204–205
Crispy buttermilk chicken,
  223
Crispy honey Dijon chicken,
  202–203
Crispy veggie rolls, 16–17
Croutons, homemade
  bagel, 39
Cucumbers
  and garlic cream cheese
    spread, 27
  sliced, in sour cream and
    garlic sauce, 8
Curry sauce, chicken with,
  Erma's, 156–157
Custard pie, 308–309

Date muffins, 28
David's ranch and dill
  pretzels, 13
Deviled eggs, 44–45
Dijon mayonnaise spread for
  sandwiches, 10
Dill and ranch pretzels,
  David's, 13

INTERNATIONAL CONVERSION CHART

These are not exact equivalents: they've been slightly rounded to make measuring easier.

LIQUID MEASUREMENTS

American	Imperial	Metric	Australian
2 tablespoons (1 oz.)	1 fl. oz.	30 ml	1 tablespoon
¼ cup (2 oz.)	2 fl. oz.	60 ml	2 tablespoons
⅓ cup (3 oz.)	3 fl. oz.	80 ml	¼ cup
½ cup (4 oz.)	4 fl. oz.	125 ml	⅓ cup
⅔ cup (5 oz.)	5 fl. oz.	165 ml	½ cup
¾ cup (6 oz.)	6 fl. oz.	185 ml	⅔ cup
1 cup (8 oz.)	8 fl. oz.	250 ml	¾ cup

SPOON MEASUREMENTS

American	Metric
¼ teaspoon	1 ml
½ teaspoon	2 ml
1 teaspoon	5 ml
1 tablepoon	15 ml

OVEN TEMPERATURES

Fahrenheit	Centigrade	Gas
250	120	½
300	150	2
325	160	3
350	180	4
375	190	5
400	200	6
450	230	8

WEIGHTS

US/UK	Metric
1 oz.	30 grams (g)
2 oz.	60 g
4 oz. (¼ lb)	125 g
5 oz. (⅓ lb)	155 g
6 oz.	185 g
7 oz.	220 g
8 oz. (½ lb)	250 g
10 oz.	315 g
12 oz. (¾ lb)	375 g
14 oz.	440 g
16 oz. (1 lb)	500 g
2 lbs.	1 kg